JOURNEY TO FREEDOM

30 DAYS TO FORGIVENESS AND HOPE

DR. RICH DORST

Unless otherwise noted, all Scriptural references are from the New International Version.

Some of the messages in this book have been inspired by Dr. Rich Dorst on his daily radio program, *Joy in the Morning*, in Palm Springs, California.

JOURNEY TO FREEDOM:
30 Days to Forgiveness and Hope

ISBN 978-0-615-44674-5
Copyright 2011 by Dr. Rich Dorst
Editors: Dr. Robert Stuart Thomson and Steve Dorst

First Published April 2011
Revised and Reprinted July 2011
Third Printing April 2012
Fourth Printing Jun 2012
Fifth Printing February 2013 (Spanish Translation)
Sixth Printing July 2013

Printed in the USA
BookMasters®, Inc.
30 Amberwood Parkway
P.O. Box 388
Ashland, OH 44805
(877) 312-3520

Introduction

Life is a journey.

Sometimes the journey is joyful, inspiring, and fulfilling. At other times it's a difficult struggle. We've all experienced winding roads and frustrating detours along the way. Everyone knows about stumbling blocks, disappointments, and losses. We all face problems and pressures, fears and frustrations, struggles and setbacks.

I've always believed it is important to be aware of what is happening in our lives and to reflect on our experiences, so that we can learn and grow as a result. That's why I wrote this book. Let me share with you how it came about.

In 2010, I experienced what I like to call a "nudge" from God to write a book that might encourage those who are going through challenging times. In less than a year, our non-profit foundation has had requests for more than 100,000 copies of *Journey to Freedom.* We have sent books to well over 100 groups comprising four different areas: prison and jail ministries, a variety of recovery and rehabilitation programs, members of our military services, and what I like to call multi-faceted ministries - groups such as the Coachella Valley Rescue Mission in Indio, California and the Neighborhood Christian Center in Memphis, Tennessee. These groups offer a full range of caring ministries, such as providing food, shelter, job training, discipleship, evangelism, medical and legal assistance, etc.

Since this book was first printed in April, 2011, I've discovered that most of us deal with the same problems and issues. We all wrestle with broken dreams and personal failure. We all have a deep longing to find hope and meaning in life.

So if you are seeking peace, purpose, forgiveness, hope, and maybe a new beginning in life, my prayer is that *Journey to Freedom* will be helpful to you.

The title has been carefully chosen: *Journey to Freedom: 30 Days to Forgiveness and Hope.* Why 30 days? Because that seems to me to be a reasonable period of time to accomplish significant life-changes. Not long before I finalized the first printing of this book, I laughed out loud when I came across book titles that promised change in much shorter time. One promised "A New You by Friday"! Another said we could revolutionize our lives in 60 seconds!

I wish it were that easy, but let's be realistic. I'm not offering a quick fix. In real life, change takes time and a great deal of effort. To me, 30 days – one month – seems believable as a good start.

I sincerely believe – and pray – that as you read this book, you will experience freedom, forgiveness, and peace. It may take a month. It may take longer. Or it may happen sooner. But I do believe that if you try, you can take giant strides on your journey – provided you approach it with an open mind and heart.

For me, faith was indeed a journey. I wasn't raised in the Christian faith. Although I am a minister, I never even stepped inside a church until I was 15. And the only reason I did so at that time was to play basketball at a large church in downtown Pittsburgh, Pennsylvania! I guess I believed in a God, but to be perfectly honest, He was nothing more than "just a word" to me. But over time, I began to understand that God could be personal and real. A few years later, I made a faith commitment that revolutionized my life. If you are looking for a meaningful relationship with your Creator, I hope that the messages of this book will be helpful on *your* spiritual journey.

Every author brings a particular slant or focus to his or her writing. Let me share the two main principles underlying this book.

First, I believe that we can't even begin to comprehend the magnitude of God's love toward us!

Though some people see God as a stern and angry judge, this is not the God of the Bible. The God I have experienced has communicated His love to us in the person of His Son, Jesus Christ, who walked this planet as one of us. He was tempted, and He experienced our struggles. Jesus accompanies us in life! He hurts when we hurt, and He offers to give us strength and guidance in our journey, which often can be so difficult.

Second, I believe that faith means trusting God, putting our cares and concerns – in fact, our whole lives – in His hands.

If you have a hard time doing this, I hope *Journey to Freedom* will help you.

I invite you to think about the following when you read *Journey to Freedom:*

1. **Consider reading just one chapter every day**. Resist the urge to read more. Think about each day's message in a very personal way. Ask how it applies to your life. Each chapter is very short, so if you think it would be helpful, read it again. (Maybe you'd like to take a pen or pencil and highlight certain things that you want to remember – and possibly share with others.)

2. **Reflect on the Action Step**. This is really key. I have tried to suggest specific steps for you to take each day in order to apply the life-message of that day's chapter.

3. **Think about the Bible verse.** Each verse has been carefully chosen to reinforce the theme of that day's message.
4. **Finally, pray.** Prayer is simply talking to God. I've provided an appropriate prayer for each day, but you may wish to pray in your own words.

You will note that I have frequently selected quotations (or provided verses from the Bible, or my own thoughts) and highlighted them in boxes. These are not just random inspirational thoughts; each has been carefully chosen to complement the chapter which follows. The theme of the quote will always be the same as the message for the following day. So when you are ready to read a particular chapter, please be sure not to overlook the quote which precedes it.

I wish you well on your journey to freedom, forgiveness, and hope. Wherever you find yourself on your spiritual journey, find the courage to take *the next step*. A long journey begins with a single step, and yours begins on Page 1. I'm confident that God will walk with you every step of the way. The combination of God's help and your own efforts has the power to change your life!

DEDICATION

It is with deep appreciation, admiration and affection that I dedicate to Ken Wents and Marty Calhoun this sixth printing of Journey to Freedom.

My good friend, Ken Wents, recently discovered that he had an unwelcome visitor enter his body, pancreatic cancer. By the time it was diagnosed, it was too late to treat, and in a matter of months, our Lord called Ken home on May 3, 2013.

I first met Ken in 1996 when we started our church with 12 people attending a Bible study. After we became an actual congregation, Ken served as a member of our Church Council, the spiritual leaders of Community Church of Joy. Ken's wife, Gloria, was a lovely woman who, like Ken, developed cancer; God called her home just six weeks later.

Ken remained utterly devoted to Gloria, visiting her grave on a regular basis. He continued to speak of her lovingly. Many of us who knew Ken were secretly praying that God would bring another very special, godly woman into his life. And he did! Marty Calhoun. On a Super Bowl Sunday 15 years ago, friends had invited Ken to watch the game with them. He called me the very next day, sounding like a smitten teen-ager: "Brother Rich, I just met the woman I'm gonna spend the rest of my life with!" That's how Ken was – if he knew something was right, he went for it.

As I got to know Marty, I quickly knew that Ken was right: God had indeed led him and Marty to each other. She is a wonderful friend, hostess, and lover of people.

I don't think I've ever met a couple who expressed their love for their children and grandchildren the way Marty and Ken did! She had one daughter, Carre, the light of her mother's life. Likewise, he had one daughter, Sherri, of whom Ken always spoke in glowing terms. Sherri has two sons, Sean and Garrett. Before I met them, just listening to Ken brag on them, I thought: "Is it possible for these young men to be as spectacular as their grandpa thinks they are?" I immediately realized that Garrett and Sean were real super stars: good-looking, intelligent, warm, sincere, athletic, and possessed with a solid work ethic.

Marty and Ken always saw the best in people, and they brought out the best in them. This dedication is just one small way to honor this special couple who were genuine, loving, hospitable, kind, passionate about caring for people, and, above all, committed to their faith in Jesus Christ.

Table of Contents

Day 1, God Can't Remember!

How would you like to be set free from guilt? Open your heart to the message in this story, and your life just may be changed forever!

I've always loved the story about a priest who was truly a man of God, but he carried a secret burden of a sin that he had committed many years before. Nobody else knew about his transgression.

Even though he had told God he was sorry, and truly meant it, for some reason he couldn't accept God's forgiveness and he had no peace or joy – only guilt.

A woman in his congregation claimed to have visions of speaking with Christ. She felt like Jesus would tell her things that nobody else could know.

The priest, quite skeptical of her claims, challenged her: "The next time you have one of these 'visions,' I want you to ask the Lord what sin I committed while I was in seminary, 20 years ago!"

She readily agreed and went home. When she returned to the church a couple of days later, the priest said: "Well, did Jesus visit you? Did the Lord speak to you?"

"Oh, yes, Father, He certainly did!"

"Well, what did the Lord tell you?"

"He said, 'I forget, and he should, too!'"

This is what I call the wonderful forgetfulness of God! Our Creator is a loving God, not vengeful. But He is also a God of perfect justice. So when the sorrow for the wrongs we have done moves us to respond as God desires, He forgives us completely.

A verse in the Bible underscores this truth: "I bury your sins in the deepest sea and remember them no more."

I have a friend, an ex-inmate, who is also in Narcotics Anonymous. When he read this chapter, he exclaimed: "Nobody can beat me up like I can!" He's absolutely right; usually we're our own harshest critic. We need to remind ourselves often that when we confess our sins, God forgives them. And when they are forgiven, they are forgotten.

The past – the hurt, the pain, the brokenness, the self-hating – it can all be gone. We just need to fully accept the reality of the awesome forgetfulness of God.

My Action Step

Think of your regrets. Tell God you're sorry. If you're sincere, God has forgiven you. Now the question is, Are you ready to forgive yourself?

God's Encouraging Word

"If we confess our sins, he [God] is faithful and just and will forgive our sins and purify us from all unrighteousness."

—1 John 1:9

Prayer (or just pray what's on your heart)

Oh God, you know that I find it very hard to forgive myself. Though I am already paying the price for my past errors, I often still feel the need to punish myself even more. Lord, I pray that you will give me the ability to truly see you as the loving God that the Bible says you are – the God who fully forgives me of all my sins. Help me to accept your forgiveness, so that I may be able to forgive myself. When that happens, then I know that I can begin to truly be free. Amen.

Day 2, Forgiving Others

You can be freed from bitterness!

One of the most powerful words in the English language is the word "forgive." In order to grasp its meaning, it's helpful to focus on the second part of the word, "give."

To forgive means to give another person a release from the wrong that he or she did to you. It means giving up your right of retaliation. As a friend of mine once put it, forgiving means "giving up my right to hurt you for hurting me."

I find many powerful truths in the cartoon strip, "The Wizard of Id." This strip was created in 1964 by Brant Parker and Jay Hart and has won numerous awards. Id is a run-down and depressed little kingdom in medieval times. The ruler is a dwarfish little fellow known only as "King," but also called "Sire" by his subjects and his court.

One day the king is bemoaning all the bad things that people are saying about him. He is bitter and tells Rodney, his chief knight, that he can never forgive these people!

Rodney offers some wise advice: "Sire, perhaps you should go to church." So the king and Rodney go to The Church of the Kingdom. But to the king's dismay, he spots a huge sign outside of the church announcing the sermon for that day, "Why You *Must* Forgive!"

The king's reaction is priceless. He turns to Rodney and asks: "What do you suppose is playing at the Methodist Church?"

Nobody ever said that forgiveness was easy!

Forgiving those who have wronged us is easier said than done. But it is much healthier to forgive than to continue harboring bitterness and resentment. When we refuse to forgive, we're putting ourselves in a prison. It's like we're drinking a poisonous potion that eats away at our insides.

Yesterday's chapter talked about the importance of accepting God's forgiveness and forgiving ourselves. But we can't stop there. Once we're forgiven and free, we then need to reach out and release the person who wronged us. Forgiveness is always within our power. *Forgiving is a choice.*

My Action Step

In the Lord's Prayer, Jesus says that in order to be forgiven, we must be willing to forgive! Are you? Think of a person right now you can release from the wrong they did to you. Forgive them today!

God's Encouraging Word

"If you forgive others for the wrongs they do to you, your Father in heaven will forgive you. But if you don't forgive others, your Father will not forgive your sins." – Matthew 6:14-15, *Contemporary English Version*

Prayer (or just pray what's on your heart)

Heavenly Father, when I feel I have been wronged or hurt by someone, the pain and anger in my heart are difficult to forget. Only you, Lord, can help me to release my hurtful feelings, and I ask that you help me to forgive others for any wrongs I feel have been inflicted on me. I ask this in the name of your Son, who showed us the true meaning of forgiveness. Amen.

Day 3, Dealing with Loneliness

If a survey were taken asking people which personal problems concerned them the most, loneliness would be at or near the top of the list. How can you overcome loneliness?

You may remember the Beatles' remarkably popular tune of the 1960s, *Eleanor Rigby*. I've always been amazed by its popularity, because the message of the song is not what you would call upbeat or uplifting.

It's about people who suffer loneliness and isolation:

> *Ah, look at all the lonely people....*
> *All the lonely people, where do they come from?*
> *All the lonely people, where do they all belong?*
> *Eleanor Rigby died in the church and was buried along with her name.*
> *Nobody came.*
> *Father McKenzie wiping the dirt from his hands*
> *as he walks from the grave.*
> *No one was saved.*

My guess is that this song did so well because we all fear loneliness and isolation.

Nobody is immune. One day Elvis Presley had a common cold. One of his staff asked him, "Hey, Elvis, how ya' feelin'?" The king of rock and roll answered, "Alone." He was the most famous singer of his day. He was surrounded by adoring fans and an entourage of people. Yet Elvis Presley felt lonely.

Not long ago I ran across an acquaintance at the post office. He'd been married for 52 years when his wife suddenly became ill and died. Bob hasn't been the same since! His wife was the love of his life and his best friend. Like Elvis, my friend felt alone.

Are you lonely?

Loneliness can be a terrible affliction. It can be a prison. Some people who are lonely simply don't know how to escape. They don't reach out to God or to other people and, often, when others reach out to them, they aren't receptive.

When you come face to face with loneliness, I encourage you to do two things. I guarantee they will work for you – provided you work at it!

Step One: Let God be your friend and personal companion

I find great personal comfort and have provided encouragement to people over the years by focusing on the verse in which God promises: "I will never leave you nor forsake you" (Joshua 1:5). If you develop a growing relationship with God, His promise will become a source of comfort: you will have the confidence that the Lord's presence is always with you.

You may not have been a particularly spiritual person up to this point. Maybe you've struggled with the idea of a personal God or having Jesus Christ impact your life. The wonderful news is that regardless of your past relationship or lack of relationship with your Creator, you can turn to Him right now and ask Him to fill the empty parts of your heart and soul. God will never judge you for your past. He only cares about your today and all your tomorrows.

Step Two: Open yourself up to other people

Don't shut yourself away from others. Most of us do such a good job of covering up our personal pain that even people who know us well and love us unconditionally aren't aware that we are lonely. Often, the important people in our lives are the ones who can convey hope and meaning to us when we're lonely and depressed.

My Action Step

If you find the courage to take these two steps, while the road may not be easy, you can experience meaning, peace and joy in relationship with God and other people. Of course you may feel lonely in the future – you're only human – but you'll never have to be *overwhelmed* by loneliness ever again! So decide right now that you'll do your very best to open up to God and other people.

God's Encouraging Word

"God has assured us, 'I'll never let you down, never walk off and leave you.'" – Hebrews 13:5, *The Message*

Prayer (or just pray what's on your heart)

Father, help me to break down the wall that I have built around myself and my emotions. I need you in my life and in my restless heart to fill my lonely places. More than that, Lord, help me to reach out to other lonely people. Help me to let them know of your unending love and comfort. Amen.

"Eleanor Rigby" was written by Paul McCartney and John Lennon, Sony Beatles Ltd; Sony/ATV Tunes LLC

"When the world says, 'Give up!' God whispers, 'Try it one more time.'" – Anon

Day 4, Hold On to Your Dreams!

You may be in a difficult place right now, but one day, new doors will be open for you to walk through. You don't have to walk through them by yourself; God will walk with you. Don't let your dreams die!

At some point, I think just about everybody has been tempted to give up, to throw in the towel.

Don't do it; treasure your dreams, and work so they come true!

Life can be very difficult. Stresses can mount up. Sometimes it's hard to see the light at the end of the tunnel.

You may feel like that right now. If you do, I want to offer you some encouragement. Countless individuals have faced difficult times and, through faith, determination and perseverance have emerged victorious. Think about these famous "failures" who overcame their failings and made their dreams come true.

Michael Jordan

Perhaps the greatest basketball player who ever lived, "Air Jordan" was cut from his high school team. He later said, "I've failed over and over again in my life. That's why I succeed."

Jerry Seinfeld

The first time Seinfeld walked on-stage at a comedy club, he looked out at the audience and froze. He stumbled through his material and was booed offstage. But the following night he returned, and when he finished, the crowd gave him a standing ovation!

The Beatles

Decca Records chose not to offer a recording contract to the Beatles. An executive said: "We don't like their sound. Groups with guitars are on their way out."

Elvis Presley

In 1954, Jimmy Denny, manager of the Grand Old Opry, fired Elvis after just one performance. He told the King of rock and roll: "You ain't goin' nowhere, son. You oughta go back to drivin' a truck!"

Vincent Van Gogh

Guess how many paintings Van Gogh sold during his lifetime. One! It was sold for the equivalent of about $50 (in today's dollars) to the sister of a friend. But this lack of recognition didn't keep Van Gogh from pursuing his dream. He completed more than 800 paintings. Recently, one of his paintings, *Portrait of Dr. Cachet,* sold for $82.5 million.

Walt Disney

Disney was fired by a newspaper editor because he "lacked imagination and had no good ideas." [I wonder if this editor has ever heard of Disneyland!]

Charles Schultz

Would you believe that every cartoon this world-famous creator of the "Peanuts" cartoon strip submitted to his high school yearbook staff was rejected? By the way, Walt Disney wouldn't hire him!

Abraham Lincoln

Abe Lincoln failed in business. He was forced to file for bankruptcy. Abe turned to politics but experienced defeat after defeat. He couldn't get elected to the legislature, to Congress, to the Senate or to the vice-presidency. Every two years or so he suffered a heart-breaking setback, causing him to write in a letter to a friend: "I am now the most miserable man living."

These are inspiring stories about determined, successful people. They failed, as we all do; but they refused to allow their dreams to be derailed. You can bet that even when Abe Lincoln couldn't get elected to public office, he continued pursuing his passion to serve the people, just for the joy of it. And Elvis and the Beatles loved making music and wouldn't give up.

We can learn something from the experiences of these famous "failures." While it is true that you may entertain certain dreams which you can't fulfill *right now*, don't let go of your dreams!

Life teaches us that new doors will be open for you to walk through. Have faith in God. Never let your dreams die!

My Action Step

Everybody fails sometime. Nobody is a winner all the time. We just have to learn to maintain confidence and faith in the face of failure. *Put all your confidence in Jesus Christ,* and you will be able to say, "I can do everything through Christ who gives me strength" (Philippians 4:13).

God's Encouraging Word

"We often suffer, but we are never crushed. Even when we don't know what to do, we never give up. In times of trouble, God is with us, and when we are knocked down, we get up again." – 2 Corinthians 4:8-9, *Contemporary English Version*

Prayer

Lord, I have failed countless times, and sometimes it's hard to keep a positive outlook about the future. My present situation wears on me, and it prevents me from pursuing some of my dreams. I ask you to give me more and more faith in Jesus Christ so that I might learn and grow from my past failures and make progress toward my hopes and dreams in the future. Amen.

Notes

Day 5, "God Don't Make No Junk!"

Are you a "nobody" or a "somebody" who really matters?

Some years ago a lady visited the church where I was pastor. After the service she came up and asked if she could make an appointment to talk with me. This was a bit unusual, because it was her first visit. But there was an obvious sadness to her that made me immediately say "sure."

A day or two later she came to my office. Her name was Maggie. In an effort to get to know her, I asked her about herself. She slumped in her chair with a miserable look on her face and said without any emotion: "Thank you so much for taking the time to talk to me. I know that I'm not important, but ...."

Her words faded off into a heart-rending silence. I responded: "You *are* important! You're special to God. He loves you with a love that we can't even comprehend. Maggie, you're a unique *somebody* – you're a child of God!"

I wish I could tell you that my spiritual "pep talk" immediately transformed this woman, but that wouldn't be the truth. But it did have *some* effect. Our talk was an important first step. With my encouragement, she began meeting with a counselor. Over time she began to believe that she really did matter in this world. That she was a "somebody."

To this day, Mahalia Jackson remains one of America's most famous Gospel singers. Born in 1911 to a very poor family in New Orleans, Jackson's father was a Baptist minister who supplemented his income by cutting hair and unloading cargo. Her mother was a maid who unfortunately died when Mahalia was just five.

Living in New Orleans, Mahalia soaked up the blues and jazz. She sang at the inauguration of John F. Kennedy and for Billy Graham. She sang to millions of people via television. But Mahalia Jackson reached the pinnacle of her career when she sang for Dr. Martin Luther King, Jr., when Dr. King gave his famous, "I Have a Dream," speech.

While serving at a church in Memphis, Tennessee, in the 1980s, I had the pleasure of working with Lane Adams, formerly part of Billy Graham's evangelistic team. Lane said that Mahalia once told him, "God don't make no junk!"

Don't you love that? *God don't make no junk!* That's what I was trying to communicate to Maggie.

So how do you see yourself? As a "nobody" or as "somebody" who really matters? In spite of how much we've blown it in the past, regardless of how much punishment we've inflicted on ourselves, this remains true: God don't make no junk!

My Action Step

Like Maggie, Mahalia, and me, you're a special person, because you are the object of God's love. *You really matter to God!* When you take a step of faith and enter His spiritual family, you can have an exciting future and experience the joyful life Christ offers to those who follow Him.

God's Encouraging Word

"You created my inmost being; you knit me together in my mother's womb. I praise you because I am fearfully and wonderfully made." – Psalm 139:13-14a

Prayer

God, thank you for seeing me as special. Thank you for making me feel that I really matter to you! May this unconditional love become the strong foundation of my life – so that I can love and accept myself and love and accept others, as well. Please remind me of this when I'm down – that your love never fails. Amen.

Notes

"Let God's promises shine on your problems."
– Corrie Ten Boom

Day 6, Messing Up Doesn't Mean It's Forever!

Have you ever wondered if being sorry is enough? Is anything more needed?

A few years ago, there was a preacher who lived in a town in rural California. Like many people, he'd made a serious mistake in his past. One day, some members of his congregation who held a grudge against him discovered his mistakes and wrote him a letter, threatening to reveal all the sordid details of his past.

What would you do if you were in his shoes? Confront the letter-writers? Bargain with them to keep quiet?

This is what he did. The very next Sunday, he read the letter to the congregation, word-for-word. He told them that the allegations were absolutely true. And then he added: "Through Jesus Christ I know that I have been forgiven. Through God's love, I have put the past behind me and I have become a new man."

Simon Peter can relate. He was the best-known disciple of Jesus Christ. Peter was a fisherman and a strong, outgoing fellow. He always talked a good game, but all too often it was just words. His "walk" didn't match his "talk."

Peter's greatest failing came on the heels of his greatest boast. Peter told Jesus that, even if all His other disciples might leave Him, he *never* would. But then, after Jesus was arrested, Peter's cowardice became evident. He denied that he even knew who Jesus was! Not once, but three times, Peter lied about his allegiance to Jesus.

Upon the third denial, just as Jesus had predicted, the rooster crowed. The sounds of the rooster brought Peter to his senses. Realizing what he had done, he went off by himself and cried bitterly. He realized what a coward he was and how he'd failed Jesus. He was sorry, but was being sorry enough?

How could Peter live with himself after that? Would he be able to accept Jesus' forgiveness? Would Peter be able to forgive *himself*? These are the sorts of questions that we *all* have to face at one time or another.

Fortunately, Peter had an encounter with Jesus after the resurrection. The Lord appeared to all the disciples, including Peter. But He focused on Peter, because he was the one who had blown it by denying Jesus. Jesus lovingly forgave Peter and then showed He trusted him again by commissioning him to become a leader of the Church in Jerusalem.

We all have issues from our past that we're not proud of. We all need forgiveness and a new beginning, just like the California pastor and Simon Peter. Both knew that they had done wrong. But they also arrived at a place in their lives where they could say: "In spite of what I've done, the Lord still loves me and stands ready to forgive me!"

How about you? Have you come to that place? It's worth pursuing, because God's forgiveness is absolutely life-changing!

My Action Step

Take a moment by yourself. Confess your sins openly and specifically to God. Be honest about them. God *promises* to forgive you!

God's Encouraging Word

"For God so loved the world that he gave his one and only Son, that whoever believes in him shall not perish but have eternal life. For God did not send his Son into the world to condemn the world, but to save the world through him."

– John 3:16-17

Prayer

Jesus, you loved me enough to die on the cross for my sins. You took the penalty and punishment which I deserve. Right now, I place my faith in who you are and what you did, as complete payment for my sins. Thank you for giving me forgiveness and a new beginning. I accept your gift by confessing my failures, sins, and shortcomings to you daily. Thank you for saving me and giving me a new beginning. Amen.

Notes

"When you say a situation or a person is hopeless, you're slamming the door in the face of God." – Charles L. Allen

Day 7, God Isn't Finished With You Yet!

The Lord is incredibly patient with us! We might grow frustrated with our performance or with another person, but God is different. His patience and mercy are beyond anything we can imagine.

Do you ever feel frustrated with yourself? Disappointed that your actions didn't follow your inner desires? Maybe you did everything you could to make a relationship work, but the other person said that it wasn't enough.

I think of times when I haven't put my money where my mouth is – when my "walk" didn't follow my "talk." Ever feel like that? Welcome to the human race!

On those occasions when I feel like I've "blown it," or didn't do as well as I should have, I've learned to stop condemning myself. Now I follow another plan: I just say to myself (and sometimes to other people as well): *Please be patient ... God isn't finished with me yet!*

God is pictured in the Bible as a great potter. I've been to Israel, the land of the Bible, 16 times and have been mesmerized while watching the potter at his wheel. His tools are quite simple – a stone at the bottom, a vertical axle and another stone on the top. The potter sits and spins the bottom stone with his feet while at the same time working the clay atop the upper stone. At times the clay doesn't yield itself to the fingers of the potter – usually because of impurities in the clay. What's the potter to do? No problem. He simply removes the impurities and continues fashioning the clay.

Sometimes I feel like I'm a lot like imperfect clay. I don't always cooperate with the moving fingers of the potter – Almighty God – in my life. And sometimes, like the clay, my life becomes bent, broken or cracked.

Thank God, He doesn't throw me away! He keeps working me, shaping me into something beautiful and useful.

Please be patient ... God isn't finished with me yet!

Let me tell you the story about a great sculptor who followed in the footsteps of his father. When the father was in his 80's, he went to live with his son. He'd work with the clay every day, but his fingers were not as nimble as when he was young. His eyes failed him. Every evening, when he looked at what he had made, he'd go to bed, utterly discouraged.

One night while his father slept, the son took his father's clay and reworked it. Then, in the morning, the father came down the stairs, looked at the work of art and exclaimed: "Why, it's not so bad after all!"

That's a compelling parable of what God can do for us! The divine potter can take our efforts – which are usually far short of perfect – and mold them into something that's useful and quite beautiful.

Be humble, not defensive. Work to improve yourself, being honest with yourself, others and God along the way.

So the next time you disappoint yourself or someone you care about or someone points out the flaws in your "clay," rather than condemning yourself, just say to that person: *Please be patient ... God isn't finished with me yet!*

My Action Step

Make a list of the things you don't like about yourself. Be specific, but don't beat yourself up. Which ones are you working on? Pick just one thing you can do to improve yourself, and begin implementing that change today.

God's Encouraging Word

"The Lord is merciful and compassionate, slow to get angry and filled with unfailing love. The Lord is good to everyone; he showers compassion on his creation." – Psalm 145:8-9, *New Living Translation*

Prayer

Lord, thanks for your love and patience. I confess that sometimes I mess up my life, and I ask for your help and strength, that I might walk in your ways and do your will. Amen.

Notes

"Hope is putting faith to work when doubting would be easier." – Anon

Day 8, How Much Faith is Enough?

Do you believe in God and trust in His promises for your life? Are you a bit like the father in this story, who admitted that part of him believed in Jesus and part of him didn't?

A minister, a priest, and a rabbi sat discussing the ideal position for prayer while a telephone repairman worked nearby. The minister stated his view, "Kneeling is definitely best."

"No way," the rabbi countered: "I get the best results standing with my hands outstretched to heaven."

"You're both wrong," the priest insisted. "The most effective prayer position is lying prostrate, face down on the floor."

Overhearing this conversation, the telephone repairman could no longer contain himself. "Hey, fellas," he interrupted: "the best prayin' I ever did was hangin' upside down from a telephone pole!"

Many of us can relate to that. Prayer has the most impact when we are most in need of God's help. When we feel helpless, powerless. When we realize how inadequate we are and how much we need to rely on God's power and goodness. Prayer is talking with God, and part of becoming a stronger Christian is praying during both the bad times and the good times – and being honest and open with God.

There's a great story in the Bible about a father whose son was quite ill, both mentally and physically. His body often would go into convulsions. He rolled around on the ground and foamed at the mouth. It was a tragic situation that he lived with, every day of his life. The boy's father had spent all of his money on doctors but with no success. He approached Jesus, who was becoming known as a great healer, sent by God. So this man humbled himself and cried out to Jesus: "If you can do anything, have compassion on us and help us" (Mark 9:22). Jesus told him: "All things are possible for the one who believes" (v.23), and He asked this father if he believed.

The man could have lied. Maybe he thought long and hard about tricking Jesus by exaggerating the reality of his faith. But instead, he answered honestly, "I believe; help my unbelief" (v. 24). What this man was saying is that he had belief at the center and unbelief around the edges. Or maybe it was the other way around. Either way, part of him believed, and part of him had a hard time believing.

What I take from this story is that God is willing to hear and answer our prayers, even when we admit that our faith is lacking! As long as we're seeking God and are honest with Him, that's enough. In this man's case, Jesus saw that his faith was real and healed his son.

Where do *you* need faith today?

My Action Step

We don't need "perfect" faith in order for God to work in our lives. Why don't you take a step of faith right now and begin to trust God with one area of your life you struggle with? You will then find that your faith will grow, as you learn more about God, who He is, and what He is like.

God's Encouraging Word

"Jesus replied, if you have faith as small as a mustard seed, you can say to this mulberry tree, 'Be uprooted and planted in the sea,' and it will obey you." – Luke 17:6 [The mustard seed is the smallest of all seeds. Several hundred will fit in the palm of your hand.]

Prayer

Jesus, I can identify with the father in the story that you told. Sometimes I feel like I really believe, but then at other times I find myself doubting. Thank you for not rejecting me when I struggle. Please work in my heart so that I may come to a place of confident faith in you – a faith that can help me to overcome life's storms. Amen.

Notes

"When we put our cares in God's hands, He puts his peace in our hearts." – Verenise Velasquez

Day 9, Letting Go –
A Prelude to Adventure

You'll open yourself up to all sorts of amazing experiences if you learn to place your fears on God's shoulders, instead of your own.

On my 50th birthday, some friends gave me a shocking gift – a certificate for a parachute jump from 14,000 feet! I didn't know how to react! I had never – not for a single moment – entertained the notion of jumping out of an airplane!

I wasn't so sure that I wanted to do this! I gave it a lot of thought. Finally, I decided that I didn't want to disappoint those who gave me this gift, so I decided to give it a go.

The day came. I received about 30 minutes of instruction from a trained parachutist, and then the plane took off. It was a tandem jump. I was strapped to the instructor. But I was deathly nervous. As we climbed to 12,000 feet, then 13,000, 14,000, my mouth became more and more dry. It felt like my mouth was stuffed with cotton! When the door opened, I took a deep breath, put my foot on the metal stand, and we dove out into the unknown.

At first, it felt just like diving into a swimming pool, but what my instructor forgot to tell me was that I would do an immediate backward somersault! I almost lost my lunch, right then and there! I'm thinking to myself: "What's gonna happen *next* that he forgot to tell me?" We were falling so fast that I froze. My mind was numb. It was like I was trapped in a wind tunnel, with a violent wall of sound boxing me in. The world was falling at me at a thousand miles per hour.

But then I found a groove, a smooth, controlled fall, like a pillow of air. I looked down to see the purple and sand-colored mountains of Palm Springs, California, stretching as far as the eye can see. For a moment, I was the only person in the world with that view. How cool is that!

As the earth came faster, I was suddenly aware of how quickly I was falling, and I experienced a second great surprise: the parachute deployed and jerked us back toward the airplane. I was a yo-yo on a string, utterly out of control.

Hmmm ... was I really sure that taking this jump was the right decision?

My answer was a resounding "Yes!" I kept thinking of my trusted friends who believed I could do this - in spite of my mild fear of heights. When our descent slowed, I felt an awesome sense of peace come over me. I was in awe at the beauty around me. Soon, I spied my family and friends who looked like ants on the ground below. And then, before I knew it, I made a safe landing.

Someone ran up to me and asked, "How was it? Did you like it? Was it scary?" Without even thinking, I found myself instinctively saying that I wanted to do it again, right then! And as I spoke the words, I surprised even myself.

Jumping out of that plane was scary, but it was also exciting! It was a challenge, an adventure. I did it! And when I did it, I experienced a rush, a high like I hadn't had in a long time.

I never would have had this amazing experience had I not been willing to let go of my fears.

This same principle applies to God in our lives. We all want to run our own lives, but if we just give God the opportunity, He can work wonders. We just need to learn to let go and trust, to base our lives on God's principles instead of our own feelings.

My Action Step

When you hold onto the past and old ways of doing things, you prevent yourself from experiencing new and exciting adventures. The greatest new experience you can ever have is a life-changing relationship with God who created you. Let go of the past. Let go of your need to control your life. Reach out to God who loves you by learning more about His truth, as found in the Bible. It may not be easy. It'll take strength and courage, but the payoff is well worth the effort!

God's Encouraging Word

"Anyone who belongs to Christ has become a new person. The old life is gone; a new life has begun." – 2 Corinthians 5:17, *New Living Translation*

Prayer

Jesus, I've tried my "old way" of doing things, and often that hasn't worked out very well. Please give me the courage to explore what it means to have a personal relationship with you. Amen.

Notes

The Bible is the only Book that satisfactorily answers the questions: "Where did I come from? Why am I here? Where am I going?" – Anon

Day 10, The Bible

If you want to anchor your life to something that will never let you down, The Bible is that anchor!

The Pentagon. September 12, 2001. What a nightmare to have to clean up! In 120-degree heat, workers struggled their way through the wreckage left behind after terrorists flew American Airlines flight #77 into the massive building.

The rescue workers didn't find any survivors, but they did make a remarkable discovery. *USA Today* reported (September 13, 2001) that on the second floor, right next to where the jet sheared off a huge portion of the building, a thick, open book remained undisturbed on a stool. It was a Bible. It wasn't burned at all. The leader of the recovery team said: "I'm not as religious as some, but this got to me. I just can't explain it!"

I was moved when I read this account, because the Bible has been for me (as it has for millions of people) the one thing that has survived every fire of my life. Everything else may be taken away, but God's Word remains true and always survives the fire. "Heaven and earth will pass away, but my words will never pass away" (Luke 21:33).

We don't really need an event like the hit on the Pentagon to "authenticate" the Bible. The evidence that the Bible is a unique book, truly God's revelation to us, is overwhelming. The Scriptures were written in three different languages by more than 40 authors over a period of 2,000 years. Imagine how people's concepts of truth and morality changed over that time span. And yet the Bible has a unified message. It tells of the same God; the same concept of sin; the same teaching of forgiveness, of heaven, of right and wrong.

Every time archaeologists have dug up something ancient that's been described in the Bible, it has validated what the Bible said. This is especially impressive when you consider that some artifacts and sites in question are mentioned nowhere else but in the Bible.

And hundreds of Biblical prophecies (predictions of events that will happen in the future), most of them written hundreds of years before the fact, have been fulfilled to the finest detail. No Biblical prophecy has ever been proven to be wrong. No other book in history can make these kinds of claims.

Yet for many of us, what matters most is that the Bible has proven to be God's word *in people's lives,* over and over again. God's Word never fails. God's promises are true; His directions work. The Bible is the rock that never moves, the compass that's never wrong, the life preserver that never sinks.

My Action Step

You may own a Bible. Are you reading it? I encourage you to read a portion of the Bible every day. Take just five-ten minutes, and really think about what you're reading. Just as I hope you're doing with this book, ask God to make the Bible's message real and practical to your everyday life. Create your own Action Step, based upon the Biblical teaching. And finally, say a brief prayer asking for God's insight and help to live out the truths that you discover. If you take God's Word seriously, it has the potential to change your life!

God's Encouraging Word

"Heaven and earth will pass away, but my words will never pass away." – Mark 13:31

"Your Word is a lamp to my feet and a light for my path." – Psalm 119:105

Prayer

Jesus, your Word has never let me down. It is truth and it is light. Open my eyes, my heart and my mind to read the Bible faithfully and accept your truth to guide me along my journey. Amen.

Notes

"You cannot escape the responsibility of tomorrow by evading it today." – Abraham Lincoln

Day 11, "Not My Fault!"

Do you sometimes blame others for your mistakes? Do you ever blame God for things you did? Growing up means learning to take full responsibility for your actions.

On Sunday, November 28, 2010, the Buffalo Bills took on the heavily-favored Pittsburgh Steelers. After a terrible first half, Buffalo fought back and took the game into overtime.

On the first possession, wide receiver Stevie Johnson, having beaten the Steeler defensive back in the end zone, dropped a perfectly-thrown pass. Instead of ending the game, with Johnson the hero, the Bills ended up punting. Pittsburgh then won the game, 19-16, after they drove down the field and kicked a field goal.

What happened to this normally sure-handed receiver, who just the week before had caught three touchdown passes? According to Johnson, it wasn't his own hands that prevented him from making the catch, and it wasn't the secondary of the Steelers, who were clearly beaten by Johnson on the play.

It was God's fault.

Johnson tweeted on the Internet after the game: "I praise you 24/7, and this is what you do to me!! You expect me to learn from this??? I'll never forget this! Ever!"

Stevie Johnson refused to accept blame. *God was responsible!!*

Or think about these phony excuses given by people who had been in car accidents. According to a UPI news release, the Metropolitan Life Insurance Company received the following explanations for accidents from its policyholders:

- "An invisible car came out of nowhere, struck my car, and vanished."

- "As I reached an intersection, a hedge sprung up, obscuring my vision."

- "The telephone pole was approaching fast. I attempted to swerve out of its path when it struck my front end."

This is the attitude of so many people in our society today. Nobody wants to accept responsibility for their actions. But we all know that sometimes we *are* responsible. Sometimes it *is* our fault.

God, in His love, is most willing to forgive us. But He also asks us to be honest and to confess our shortcomings and acknowledge the hurts that we have caused others. As human beings, we have freedom of choice, and we can't weasel out of responsibility by blaming God or other people. We need to shoulder the responsibility ourselves.

Bottom line: we need to take full responsibility for our actions and not shift the blame onto God or anyone else.

My Action Step

If you want to be whole and to have a clear conscience before God and other people, you need to accept responsibility for your actions. Alcoholics Anonymous has an excellent method for achieving this. It is found in two of their famous twelve steps:

> Step 5, Integrity – Admit to God, to ourselves and to another human being the exact nature of our wrongs.

> Step 10, Perseverance – Take personal inventory and when we are wrong, promptly admit it.

Take a moment, won't you, and with an open mind and heart decide to implement these action steps into your life, beginning right now.

God's Encouraging Word

"God wants us to grow up, to know the whole truth and tell it in love." – Ephesians 4:14, *The Message*

Prayer

Loving Jesus, you did not run away from the awesome responsibility of the cross. You went there to die for me. May I with honesty and truthfulness take responsibility for my actions. Help me to be open and honest with you and others, acknowledging my failures and trusting in your love and forgiveness. Amen.

Notes

"There is a God-shaped vacuum in every heart."
– Blaise Pascal

"No God, no peace. Know God, know peace."
– Anon

Day 12, Changing Directions

Have you ever been lost? It can be frustrating or truly frightening. What do you do when you're lost and can't find your way?

Ross Fichtner has an amusing story to tell. It happened in his first game as a defensive back for the Minnesota Vikings in 1964.

The Vikings were playing the San Francisco 49ers. The 49er quarterback, John Brodie, completed a short pass to the wide receiver, who was hit right away, causing him to fumble. The ball bounced into Jim Marshall's hands. He took off running as fast as he could, but in the confusion he got himself turned around and began running toward the wrong end zone! In an amazing role reversal, the 49er players began to block *for* Jim, keeping his teammates at bay until he reached his own end zone. When he threw the ball out of the end zone, it was recorded as a safety and two points for the 49ers! The play ended with a few 49ers patting Jim Marshall on the back!

Ross (now a staff member for The Fellowship of Christian Athletes) uses this story to illustrate the truth that *you can have all the enthusiasm and ability in the world, but if you're going in the wrong direction, the end result will be disastrous!*

The Bible tells about a brilliant Jew named Saul who was also going the wrong way. He constantly boasted about his religious accomplishments and was obsessed with keeping every detail of the Jewish law. And Saul cruelly persecuted members of a new group who called themselves "the Way" (Christians). The Bible records an instance when Saul stood by and calmly watched as his associates stoned a Christian, Stephen, to death.

41

Then one day, out of the blue, Jesus Christ turned Saul of Tarsus around! It happened while Saul was on his way to arrest Christians in the city of Damascus. Suddenly, Jesus appeared to him in a heavenly vision and spoke to him. Saul was so astonished that he fell to the ground and was temporarily blinded. From this point on, his life turned around 180 degrees. This chief persecutor of Christians was given a new name, Paul, and proceeded to devote his life to following God's will and pointing others to faith in Christ. His achievements were unparalleled. He recruited thousands of followers over 20 years, and made four major voyages around the Mediterranean, spreading the Good News of God's love throughout the ancient world. He also became the most prolific of all the writers who contributed to the New Testament.

Many people believe (or, at least hope) that they'll be right in God's sight based on their own goodness. They express it many different ways: "I've tried to live a good life." "I did the best I could." "I've never deliberately hurt anybody." "I go to church whenever I can." "I follow the Ten Commandments/the Golden Rule." "If God grades on a curve, I'm pretty sure I'll make it!"

These folks may be quite sincere in their attempts to earn their way to heaven, but they are sincerely *wrong.* Why do human efforts fall short? Paul makes it clear – beyond the shadow of a doubt – that "all have sinned and fall short of the glory of God" (Romans 3:23), and "the wages of sin is death" (Romans 6:23). You can climb to the top of the ladder in the world's eyes, but in God's sight that ladder is propped against the wrong wall if you're trying to enter Heaven based on your own goodness!

Here is another way to state the only two options available to you: Do you get to heaven by *doing something* or by *trusting Someone*? The Bible is clear that the only way to get to heaven is to put your trust in God's provision for your sin: Jesus Christ's suffering and death on the cross. In fact, Jesus so completely satisfied God's demand for justice that His last words on the cross were, "It is finished" (John 19:30). If doing any amount of anything could get you to heaven, then it wouldn't have been necessary for Jesus to die! But Jesus' loving, sacrificial act opens the gates of heaven to all those who put their trust in Him and receive Him by faith. That is why only Jesus could claim: "I am the way and the truth and the life. No one comes to the Father except through me" (John 14:6).

My Action Step

At this point in your journey, do you realize that your life has been headed in the wrong direction? Have you been counting on your own so-called "goodness" to get you into heaven? You can't live the Christian life until you've entered it. And all God requires for you to enter is simply to believe in Him. I ask you to prayerfully review the verses which follow and then reflect on the prayer. Ask God to draw you to faith in Christ so that you may receive His gift: eternal life.

God's Encouraging Word

"Yet to all who received him [Jesus Christ], to those who believed in his name, he gave the right to become children of God." – John 6:47

[Jesus said:] "I tell you the truth, he who believes has eternal life." – John 6:47

Prayer

Lord Jesus, I admit that I have sinned and fallen short of your standards over and over again. Thank you for dying on the cross to pay the penalty for my sins, so that I could be forgiven and have the gift of eternal life. Jesus, I believe that you died for me! I believe you rose from the dead to prove that you are God. Right now, I place my trust in you, alone, to save me. I'm not trusting my good life. I'm not relying on my best efforts. I'm not depending upon my religious activities. I'm trusting you alone, Jesus.

Help me from this day forward to grow in this new relationship with you. Please take out of my life the things that shouldn't be there and build into my life the things that should be. Thank you for the assurance of eternal life which begins the moment I believe in you. Now, Lord, I know that I can truly be free! Amen.

Notes

Day 13, Your "Dash"

When your time on this earth comes to an end, how would you like to be remembered?

In Steven Covey's best-selling book, "The Seven Habits of Highly Successful People," he invites the readers to imagine their own memorial service!   At first glance it's a strange suggestion, but I think he actually has a point. He asks: "When it comes to the end of your life, what would you like people to say about you?"

I think this suggestion is brilliant because it causes us to evaluate what is really important. Once we have that clearly in mind, we can try to live our lives in such a way that we will accomplish these priorities!

With this idea in mind, I want to share an inspiring poem, *Your Dash*, written by Linda Ellis.

It begins with a man who stands up to speak at the funeral of a friend. He notes that her tombstone has two dates on it: the date of birth and the year she died.   Whereas these dates are important milestones, what really matters is the "dash" between them

For that dash represents all the time
that she spent alive on earth
and now, only those who loved her
know what that little line is worth.
For it matters not how much we own –
the cars, the house, the cash.
What matters is how we live and love,
and how we spend our dash....

*If we could just slow down enough
to consider what's true and real,
and always try to understand
how other people feel,
And be less quick to anger
and show appreciation more,
and love the people in our lives
like we've never loved before....
So, when your eulogy's being read,
with your life's actions to rehash,
would you be proud of the things they say
about how you spent your dash?*

God created us in His image. This means that we have the ability to relate to Him on an intellectual, emotional, and spiritual level. We can make good choices. We can love. We can forgive, and we can grow in character and faith. Though you may be experiencing very difficult circumstances, I hope you agree that God has given all of us many blessings and opportunities. Are you using your gifts, talents, and blessings? Are you having a positive influence on other people?

So let me ask you very pointedly: at *your* memorial service, will you be proud of the things people say about how *you* spent *your* dash?

My Action Step

You may have done some very stupid things or made some serious mistakes or errors in judgment along the way, and now you're paying the price. But now it's time to look to the future. How do you plan to spend the rest of your days on this planet? List one or two specific things that you can do which will positively change your destiny.

God's Encouraging Word

"After David had done the will of God in his own generation, he died and was buried...." – Acts 13:36 (What a great epitaph that would be to have on your tombstone!)

Prayer

Oh God, the memories of my past are often painful. But as I look toward the future, knowing I can grow in my relationship with you, I have confidence that I can find hope, faith, and courage. Help me to accept your forgiveness, and then enable me to live my life in such a way that I will be pleased by what people say at my memorial service – about how I spent my "dash." Amen.

Notes

"We've all been broken at some point. Forgiving ourselves or another person helps us move forward." – Academy Award-winning actress, Julia Roberts; quoted in *Guideposts*, January, 2011

Day 14, Conquering Resentment

Carrying around resentment will eat you alive! Getting rid of it will give you a new lease on life.

There are a lot of ways to say it: nursing a grudge, having a bone to pick with someone, keeping score – just to name a few. But whatever phrase you use, they all describe the same thing: resentment.

Resentment is one subject we don't talk about much, which is odd because it's something we all battle. Resentment is "the elephant in the room" which we choose to walk around.

If you doubt this, ask yourself three questions. Be honest, now. See if you can say "no" with a clear conscience to each question.

1. Do you ever bring up old issues that someone has already asked your forgiveness for?

2. Is there anyone you persist in treating distantly, or whom you ignore, because you believe that he or she once slighted or hurt you?

3. Do you find yourself talking a lot about personal disappointments from days gone by?

Resentment surrounds us. Consider the following:

How many people hold on to grievances for things their spouses apologized for years ago?

How many adult children treat their elderly parents with contempt because they believe that they were ignored or otherwise abused as children?

How many still hold grudges, years later, against siblings?

There's no doubt about it, resentment is a popular pastime. But in this game, no one ever wins, and it costs a fortune in wasted time and energy. Look in the mirror and see what resentment has done to you!

When you nurse a grudge against someone, you're putting that person in prison in your mind. And guess who gets to play "jailer"? It's you! Holding a grudge makes no sense at all. (There is further irony: more often than not, the person you hold the grudge against is often unaware of your attitude and isn't bothered in the least!) Holding a grudge is a waste of time and energy. Resentment will eat you alive; it's like poison! Get rid of it! Let it go!

But how? There's no doubt, conquering resentment is easier said than done, but it is possible to overcome it.

It all begins with calling resentment exactly what it is: an unwillingness to forgive. It's not that we're *unable* to; it's that we're *not willing* to.

In my experience, prayer is the best solution.

It's staggering how many times we try to let go of resentment, only to find that we are powerless to do so. Yet as soon as we turn our need over to God in prayer, something amazing takes place: God is willing and able to carry our problem! God can give us the strength to overcome resentment. If you doubt me, give it a try. Prayer is the greatest power source in the universe!

My Action Step

Think for a few moments of those people you resent in your life. Maybe it would be helpful to write their names down. Now turn over that resentment and anger to God in prayer. God can help you conquer those emotions and put them to rest. A weight will be lifted, and you will be on the road to being free.

But then, go one step further. Take specific steps to make amends. Extend your complete forgiveness. Meet with this person and let him or her know that you have made a choice not to carry resentment around any longer, or if a meeting in person isn't possible, email or write a letter. While you realize that the other party may not be ready to reconcile with you, at least you have done everything in your power to extinguish bitterness and resentment from your life.

God's Encouraging Word
"Resentment kills a fool, and envy slays the simple."
– Job 5:2

Prayer
God, please help me to be free of any resentment that I harbor in my heart. As I let go of these feelings and sense your peace, I know I will begin to see the good in others more clearly. Amen.

Notes

"You can tell the size of your God by looking at the size of your worry list. The longer the list, the smaller your God." – Anon

Day 15, How to Win over Worry

Worry affects circulation, the heart, the glands, and the whole nervous system. I have never known anyone who died from overwork, but many who died from anxiety. – Dr. Charles Mayo, *American Mercury*

Are you a worrier? Do you know anyone who is? A popular song a few years ago encouraged people, "Don't Worry, Be Happy!" Oh, if it were only that easy, we would all do it!

I love the story about the dignified Irish clergyman, Bishop R. C. Trent, who had a morbid fear of becoming paralyzed. Often, he would pinch his arms and legs in order to reassure himself that he still had feeling in them. And when he would go to sleep, the fear of paralysis would often fill his dreams.

One evening, at a dinner party, he exclaimed: "It's happened at last! I've lost the feeling in my right leg!" Just then, the person sitting next to Bishop Trent said: "Sir, it may comfort you to know that it is my thigh that you have been pinching!" In reality, the Bishop had absolutely nothing to worry about.

And *that's how it usually is: Worry has no practical value.*

My daughter Keri once said to me: "Dad, I think worry is like a rocking chair. It will give you something to do, but it won't get you anywhere!"

Worry has a negative impact on our physical bodies. Doctors tell us that worry saps our energy, breaks down resistance to disease and wreaks havoc on our digestive organs and heart. A recent article in *USA Today* said that high anxiety in middle-age is a warning flag for future high blood pressure.

A New England doctor made a detailed study of things that his patients worried about. This is what he learned:

- 70 percent of the things people worried about never happened.
- 12 percent of people's worries concerned physical illnesses that were caused, or greatly aggravated, by emotional attitudes such as worry!
- Ten percent of the worries involved family members – who were perfectly able to look after themselves!
- So that left just eight percent of situations which actually needed some attention; but worry didn't contribute in any positive way.

The Bible offers us a wonderful invitation. It says, "Cast all your cares upon God, because he cares for you" *(1 Peter 5:7).* And this beautiful hymn tells us exactly how we can "cast our cares" upon the Lord:

What a friend we have in Jesus,
All our sins and grief's to bear …
Oh, what peace we often forfeit,
Oh, what needless pain we bear,
All because we do not carry
Everything to God in prayer.

Worry is basically a lack of faith. You don't *have to* worry; you can give your concerns over to God, in prayer. The Lord is never too busy for you. He's always listening.

My Action Step

The next time you're burdened with worry, take a moment, close your eyes and talk with God. List the things you're worried about. Be honest. God wants to give you a new perspective on your concerns, so they won't be nearly as overwhelming.

God's Encouraging Word

[Jesus said:] "Come unto me, all you who are weary and burdened, and I will give you rest." – Matthew 11:28

Prayer

"God, grant me the SERENITY to accept the things I cannot change; the COURAGE to change the things I can; and the WISDOM to know the difference." – The Serenity Prayer, a cornerstone of Alcoholics Anonymous, often attributed to Dr. Reinhold Niebuhr or Dr. Friedrich Oetinger, though there is no official agreement concerning authorship.

Notes

For the believer in Christ, God has promised to take our difficulties and bring good out of them.

"And we know that in all things God works for the good of those who love him." – Romans 8:28

Day 16, "Irregular" People

You can't solve every problem that you face, and not every relationship is able to be healed. What do you do when you face difficult situations and difficult people?

We've all been in stores where slightly damaged goods are offered at reduced prices. These items are designated "irregulars" and sold "as is." Maybe the shirt has a small imperfection in the stitching or the jacket's sizing is slightly off.

We all understand *merchandise* that's irregular, but what about people? Are there irregular *people?*

Joyce Landorf wrote a book with a very clever title, "Your Irregular Person." She points out that almost every family has at least one person who can be called irregular. They have issues, quirks, oddities. And they're no fun to be around! Believe me, in my experience as a pastor, I've seen a lot of irregular people. And yes, my extended family has its share, too!

Do you have someone in your life who drives you crazy – someone who seems to have a knack for always saying the wrong thing? Someone who's critical of you or insensitive or consistently negative?

Not long ago, I had a great conversation with a friend, Ruth, who recently retired from a bright career as a psychotherapist. We got to talking about exactly this issue. How do you deal with people – in particular, family members – who have injured or abandoned you? How do you move forward after emotional or physical abuse?

How do you cope with these irregular people?
What did Ruth tell me?

First, if there is a loss – if you no longer have contact with that person – then it's important to acknowledge the loss. Accept the situation for what it is. Should things change in the future that might bring you and this person into contact again, that's well and good. But for now, it's important to let it go and accept the way things are.

Second, acknowledge that you have no control over this situation. You are simply powerless. We all like to be in control; we like to feel that we can "make things better." And often, when we dedicate ourselves to doing something healing and loving and uplifting, we see results. But in some situations, you have to accept that you are powerless to change the other person or to change the situation or mend the relationship.

And then, **finally, come to the point of full acceptance.** A few years ago I was thinking of a couple of people in my life who frustrated me with their conduct and insensitivity. Then one day, suddenly, I had a "revelation" of sorts. It occurred to me that *some problems can be resolved and some can't.* There are some problems that I simply have to learn to live with. Once I realized this, I felt as though a huge burden had been lifted from my shoulders. With regard to these people, I learned to "let them go." I accepted that things wouldn't change. And our relationship would never be as I hoped. It's a sad situation, but I finally accepted it for what it was. That's why Romans 12:18 says, "If it is possible, as far as it depends on you, live at peace with everyone."

I hope that these three concepts from Ruth's experience will help you. They certainly have enlightened me.

God specializes in difficult projects! He is the God of the impossible. Turn your irregular people over to the Lord. I promise He will give you wisdom and guidance to learn how to cope – and more than that, to come out on the other side, a winner.

My Action Step

Accept the reality that God loves everyone, even those with "irregular" personalities! Make a list of the irregular people in your life. Try to be more patient with others and their personality quirks. Then, ask yourself, "Am I anyone's irregular person?

God's Encouraging Word

"Don't be hurtful and insult people just because they are hurtful and insult you. Instead, treat them with kindness. You are God's chosen ones, and he will bless you." – 1 Peter 3:8, *Contemporary English Version*

Prayer

Lord, bless the lives of the "irregular" people in my life. Help me to be more tolerant and understanding of their ways. You, Father, are the one who can change lives in a miraculous way. And if I'm anyone else's irregular person, please reveal that to me so that together we can work to make me a better person. Amen.

Notes

"Peace is not the absence of problems, but the presence of God." – Anon

"When we put our cares in God's hands, He puts His peace in our hearts." – Anon

Day 17, Peace of Mind

The Lord gives perfect peace to those whose faith is firm. – Isaiah 26:3, *Contemporary English Version*

Do you sometimes feel that there's more stress in today's world and less peace of mind?

Psychologists tell us that the greatest threat to peace of mind is guilt – residual guilt from something that we did or said in the past. I love the story about the guy who wrote to the IRS. "Many years ago I cheated on my income taxes," he confessed. "Enclosed is my check for $200." He intentionally didn't sign the letter. What followed was a surprising P.S. "If I *still* can't sleep, I'll send the rest!"

I think you'll agree with me, one key to experience peace of mind is to have a clear conscience. And the only way to have a clear conscience is by confessing what we've done wrong. We gain strength when we're honest and say: "What I did was wrong. Can you find it in your heart to forgive me?"

But we all know how hard it is to own up to our mistakes. You'll need a whole lot of courage and strength to acknowledge when you've blown it or hurt someone else. But when you do so, amazing things can happen! People usually are moved to respond in kind and to grant you forgiveness when you sincerely ask.

You may be thinking to yourself: What happens if I ask, but he or she isn't willing to forgive me? The thing to remember is that we can't control *them;* we are only responsible for our own decisions and actions. At least you'll have the peace of mind to know that you showed courage and did the right thing.

And then, of course, there is God's forgiveness. I've often found comfort in the image a friend shared with me many years ago. "Picture God with a giant eraser," he said. "God delights in eradicating all your mistakes and shortcomings. All you have to do is tell Him that you're truly sorry – and, of course, mean it!"

Confession is a powerful thing! You ought to try it. It may sound hard, but it's really not. Just be open with God about those things that you have done wrong, and ask for His forgiveness. Confession is an essential requirement to experiencing peace of mind and heart.

My Action Step

We're all experts at making all kinds of excuses. "I didn't mean to do it." "It was because my parents didn't raise me the right way." "I had a lousy education." While there may indeed be some truth to some of these reasons which explain what you've experienced, ultimately it comes down to a personal decision: Are you willing to acknowledge your wrongs? That you broke God's laws? That you hurt other people? After you read the Bible verse which follows, talk to God in prayer and be honest about where and how you've messed up. That's called confession, and it really works!

God's Encouraging Word

"If we confess our sins to God, he can always be trusted to forgive us and take our sins away." – 1 John 1:9, *Contemporary English Version*

Prayer

Jesus, I want to be honest with myself and honest with you. I confess that I've committed many wrong deeds in my life. [Reader, you may want to express some of them now.] I've broken your laws and, in the process, have hurt others and myself. Thank you for dying on the cross so that I might know your love and experience the forgiveness of my sins. Cleanse me thoroughly, Jesus, and help me to walk on the right path in the days ahead. Amen.

Notes

"Look at life through the windshield, not the rear-view mirror." – Boyd Baggett

Day 18, Beginning Again

All of us have "messed up" in the past. How would it feel to know that you could be offered a fresh, new beginning?

You wouldn't be human if you sometimes didn't wish that you could just start all over again!

We've all made rotten decisions. We've said and done things for which we're now ashamed. If given the opportunity, we would just blot these things off of the record!

Louisa Fletcher is the author of a clever little poem called, *The Land of Beginning.* I hope you'll find it helpful. I'm sharing just a small part of it:

> *I wish that there were some wonderful place*
> *Called the Land of Beginning Again*
> *Where all our mistakes and all our heartaches*
> *And all of our selfish grief*
> *Could be dropped like a shabby old coat by the door*
> *And never be put on again ....*
>
> *We would find all the things that we intended to do*
> *But forgot, or remembered too late;*
> *Little praises unspoken, little promises broken*
> *And all of a thousand and one things ....*
> *And it wouldn't be possible not to be kind*
> *In the Land of Beginning Again.*

Many times I've wished that I could "begin again"; how about you?

Psalm 103:5 says: "He [God] satisfies my desires with good things so that my youth is renewed like the eagle's." Why like the eagle's? The eagle is an especially powerful, handsome bird, an emblem of strength and beauty. However, the eagle held an additional significance for the Jews in the Bible. Because the eagle sheds and re-grows all its feathers every year, they viewed the eagle *as having a new life* each year.

How can you and I enjoy the gift of renewed life that the eagle symbolizes? One way is by learning how to close the gate on our past.

I first heard this expression with regard to the Culver Military Academy in Indiana. Culver has a marvelous tradition. Their graduation ceremony begins like graduations at other institutions. Each cadet walks up and shakes hands with the headmaster and others. But then, the twist: the graduates at Culver walk through an arch, and then through a gate, symbolizing their entrance into the future.

As the graduates walk through the gate, a marshal is standing there to encourage them: "Don't forget to close the gate!"

Actually, this was not a new suggestion to the cadets. These graduates understand the meaning of this little ritual quite well. At Culver Military Academy, students were often encouraged to close the gate.

Don't forget to close the gate on the mistakes you made here.
Don't forget to close the gate on the guilt you feel from the past.
Don't forget to close the gate to get rid of your grudges
and put your hurt and anger behind you.

Walk through the arch, into a glorious future – and don't forget to close the gate!

Do you need to close the gate on your past?

You can't change the past, but you *can* have a new beginning; you can start all over again. As you have seen in earlier chapters, it usually begins with accepting God's forgiveness and forgiving ourselves and others. Then, as the principles of Alcoholics Anonymous and Narcotics Anonymous emphasize, make amends wherever and however you can. Then, you can begin an exciting new future!

My Action Step

Sometimes, closing the gate – which sounds so simple – is *not* an easy thing to do. But isn't it time to put the past in the past? Let go of whatever it is that is holding you back and give as much of yourself over to God as you are able to give.

God's Encouraging Word

"I forget what is behind, and I struggle for what is ahead." – Philippians 3:13, *Contemporary English Version*

"Whoever is a believer in Christ is a new creation. The old way of living has disappeared. A new way of living has come into existence." – 2 Corinthians 5:17, *God's Word Translation*

Prayer

Heavenly Father, forgiving myself for the past is always the most difficult thing to do. But I'm learning that whenever I stumble, you are always there for me, without fail, to "catch me," forgive me and make me like new. Help me to finally close the gate on my past, knowing that I have received your gift of forgiveness and the promise of a fulfilling and peaceful new life through you. Amen

Are we destined to be depressed and victimized by the negative circumstances of our lives? Certainly not. In the Bible, God proclaims that, through faith, we are "more than conquerors!" That means that God will carry you through, He will lift you above your circumstances.

Day 19, Failure Isn't Fatal!

Everybody fails once in a while. No one is a winner all the time.

Some of us have been less-than-successful in parenting, marriage, relationships, career, or school. Some of us are paying the price for our failures. Some of our failings are obvious, while others are not so conspicuous. Nobody else knows about them; just us.

In my own life, I would love to be able to go back and relive certain experiences. If I could do that, I would make different decisions and avoid pain and hurt – for myself and others.

How about you? Is there anything in your life that eats at you, that haunts you? Are there days you would like to live over again?

The great humorist, W. C. Fields, once said, "If at first you don't succeed, try, try again. Then, quit. There's no use being a fool about it!" Fields was a comedian, so he was trying to be clever; but failure is no laughing matter.

Everybody, even people we call "famous" or "successful," knows about personal failure.

A good case in point is Albert Einstein, one of the greatest scientists and mathematicians who ever lived. You talk about a slow developer! Did you know that Einstein couldn't speak until he was four years old? And he flunked his freshman math class!

Babe Ruth is a baseball legend. He hit 714 home runs in the era of the "dead ball." Often, his home run production was more than the combined total of homers by the other team! But did you know that Babe Ruth also struck out 1,330 times

Or how about Fred Astaire, the entertainer who sang, acted, and danced his way into people's hearts worldwide. In 1932, when he was just starting out, a Hollywood talent scout had this to say about Fred Astaire's screen test: "Can't act. Can't sing. Can dance a little."

You may drop the ball. You may mess up. You may even be, in the eyes of some people, a complete failure.

But making a few failures (or even a lot!) is nothing you want to dwell on. Do your best to forget them and move on. I suggest you follow the advice of Charles Kettering, former Chief of Research at General Motors and one of America's greatest inventors. Kettering said that it's quite possible to "fail forward." He said: "I failed countless times, but I never surrendered leadership in my life to my failures. I determined always to fail forward." Charles Kettering always *learned* something from his failures.

When you fail, it can become the springboard to future successes.

We're all aware of our personal failings. A particular failure may be the reason that your life-situation is as it is today. *But what about tomorrow? With God's help, you can learn and grow from your many failures.*

I hope you'll remember this Good News: you might fail, but you're never a failure. God *never* calls you a failure, and in the final analysis, isn't God's opinion the only one that really counts? If you rely on God's love and patience, you can grow from past failures. You can "fail forward!"

My Action Step

Someone once said, "If you are going through hell, *keep going!*" The worst experiences are only temporary. Put your trust in God; ask for His help and guidance. People may let you down, but the Lord never will.

God's Encouraging Word

"Be strong. Take courage. Don't be intimidated ... because God, your God, is right there with you. He won't let you down; he won't leave you." – Deuteronomy 31:6, *The Message*

Prayer

Heavenly Father, strengthen my faith so that I can find the courage to acknowledge my personal failings. But may I never see myself as a failure, because you don't think of me that way. Thank you for forgiving me of all of my shortcomings. Help me to accept your forgiveness and grow from my failures. Amen.

Notes

God doesn't always solve our problems instantly. But He is with us in the darkest hours, and we can never escape His all-encompassing love.

Day 20, Patience

Do you struggle with impatience? Do you often become anxious and irritated when people don't act the way you would like them to or don't operate according to your exact timetable?

I love the story about two women who died on the same day and met St. Peter at the pearly gates.

Peter greeted them warmly and then suddenly, his pager beeped. The Lord needed him. So Peter excused himself, promising that he would return as soon as possible.

After a while, true to his word, Peter returned. He apologized to the women for causing them to wait.

The first woman understood: "Oh, St. Peter, think nothing of it; you are a *saint!* Besides, we are in heaven; time means nothing here – we have all eternity."

Peter thanked her and said: "There is one thing you must do before you can get into heaven: Spell 'God.'"

The woman answered, "G-o-d."

"Wonderful," Peter said. "You may now enter the kingdom of heaven."

Just then his pager went off a second time. He had to excuse himself once again because the Lord was calling for him.

When he returned he apologized to the other woman.

But this lady was not so understanding. She shouted at Peter: "I don't care if you *are* a saint! I'm sick and tired of waiting for you. When I was on earth, I had to wait for my husband and for my kids; I had to wait in the doctor's office and in the grocery store and on the freeways. When I got to heaven, I didn't think I'd have to wait around for *you!*"

"Well," St. Peter answered, "I appreciate that you have been honest and that you have told me exactly how you feel. Now there is one thing you must do before you may enter heaven."

"And what is that?" she demanded impatiently.

Peter answered, "*Spell Czechoslovakia!*"

I don't know about you, but I can kind of identify with this woman. I'm what is called a "Type A" personality. I find it really hard to wait. I'm just not a very patient person.

Do you often find that you are impatient with other people?

I've discovered that if you have faith, you can be confident that God has a plan for your life. When you trust God and His plans for you, some very practical things can happen:

- You can learn to deal with frustrations and setbacks and feel your life still has purpose.

- You won't throw in the towel. You won't give up hope. You'll strive to do your best.

- You can find the patience to deal with truly difficult realities. For example, why are you spending so much time in recovery and sometimes falling back into destructive patterns? Or why is your appeal not moving forward as quickly as you had thought it would?

Again, the solution is to put your full trust in God. Isaiah 40:31 puts it well:

> *Those who wait upon the Lord shall renew their strength;*
> *they shall soar on wings, like eagles. They shall run, and*
> *not grow weary, they shall walk, and not faint.*

Several years ago I looked death in the eye while battling cancer. When I recovered and returned to my church, I shared that Bible verse with them. Since then, it has begun to have new meaning for me. I'm learning to trust God's purposes and timing for my life. As a result of my experience, I'm working hard to become a more patient person. Now I try to *wait upon the Lord* more than ever. And when I do, it really works!

Waiting on the Lord: what exactly does it mean? I think it means taking all our irritations and frustrations and handing them over to God. The benefits of trusting the Lord are positively life-changing! Don't be like the lady who blew her top at St. Peter. Instead, do your best to trust God and follow His purposes for your life. Doing so will mean a world of difference.

My Action Step

You've tried your way. Maybe it's time to try God's way! Waiting on the Lord means trusting in God, and trusting in God means that you stop trusting in yourself. Make the courageous decision to turn the reigns of your life over to Almighty God.

God's Encouraging Word

"Trust in the Lord with all your heart; do not depend on your own understanding. Seek his will in all you do, and he will show you which path to take." – Proverbs 3:5-6, *New Living Translation*

Prayer

Heavenly Father, I want so much to believe the promise in this Bible verse! I long for success, not suffering. To prepare myself for a brighter tomorrow. Lord, help me to trust you in this process – and I know that one test of whether or not I am really trusting is if I can stop stressing so much about my current situation. Amen.

God's heart is especially tender toward the downtrodden and defeated. He knows your name, and He has seen every tear that you have shed.

Day 21, Encouragement

Do you know somebody who needs encouragement right now? How about yourself?

Ever feel sorry for yourself? If we're honest, we all feel down or discouraged sometimes.

Several years ago, I had a really lousy week. It seemed that nothing was going right. I felt discouraged, even depressed. When the mail came that day, I didn't even care about opening it. But something drew my attention to a large envelope that obviously had been addressed by a child. Upon opening it, I discovered a hand-drawn card with a fancy border around it so that it resembled an award certificate. It read: *Dear Dr. Dorst. You are the best speaker. You are funny. You are nice. Your friend, Albert!* Then he added this P.S., *I hope you can come see our church softball team play. I'm the batboy!*

Albert was the 10-year-old son of our church members and friends, Rebecca and Don. It was amazing how Albert's little card made my day!

A few years later I met Alex Haley, the gifted author who wrote the book on which the TV series, "Roots," was based. Flying from Pittsburgh to Los Angeles, I walked up to Haley, told him how much I had enjoyed "Roots," and asked for his autograph. The Pulitzer Prize-winning author smiled graciously. He asked my family name and then personalized the following greeting: "To the Dorst family, from the Roots family of Kunta Kinte." To this day, Haley's dedication and signature hang, framed, in our home. Just a few months after meeting Haley, I was intrigued by a magazine article I read about him. On his office wall was a picture of a turtle. That, in itself, was not so strange; but of all things the turtle was balancing on a fence! The caption read: "If you see a turtle perched atop a fencepost, think about it – the turtle didn't get there by itself!"

I guess not! Somebody must have lifted it there!

We all know people who need "lifting," don't we? Ask God to point out just one person who needs the gift of your encouragement. Regardless of how poorly things are going for you, you can usually find someone who needs a bit of a boost! Focus on them. Ask how they're doing. Encourage them like little Albert encouraged me. Lift a turtle (or a friend) to a new place they otherwise wouldn't be without you!

My Action Step

Often, when things aren't going well, we focus too much on ourselves and our own problems. But once we reach out to encourage someone else, not only do we help them, we help ourselves. Think of someone you know who is down. Find a way to encourage that person today.

God's Encouraging Word

"He [God] comforts us in all our troubles so that we can comfort others. When they are troubled, we will be able to give them the same comfort God has given us." – 2 Corinthians 1:3-4, *New Living Translation*

Prayer

God, when I'm down, help me to think of others. I know that when I begin to care for other people, I tend to stop feeling sorry for myself. And when I stop feeling sorry for myself, I know I will begin taking my first steps toward freedom! Amen

Day 22, Learning How to Deal with Hurt

A Christian will find it cheaper to pardon than to resent. Forgiveness saves the expense of anger, the cost of hatred, the waste of spirits. – Hannah More

Who has hurt you the most in your lifetime?

You probably can answer that one immediately. It's amazing how our minds can hang onto hurts. Most of us can remember, with vivid detail, hurtful things that happened 10, 20, even 30 years ago!

But holding onto such memories comes with a price. When we hold onto a grudge, over time hurt usually escalates into hate – and then we have real trouble.

We'll all be hurt in life; that's a fact. And so one of the most important life skills we can learn is how to deal with hurt.

What is our typical reaction when someone hurts us? Retaliation! Somebody hurt you? Well, hurt 'em back! This is exactly the way most people deal with being hurt: "Don't get mad, get even." (It was said that Ivana Trump, Donald Trump's ex-wife, declared: "Don't get mad; don't get even; *get everything!*")

There is just one problem: Revenge doesn't work! There is only one way to get over your hurt: forgiveness.

Someone has defined forgiving as "giving up my right to hurt you for hurting me." Think about that one for awhile: "Giving up my right to hurt you for hurting me."

When you forgive someone, you offer them a new beginning, a fresh start.

When God forgives us, He offers us a new beginning. God holds out His hand and says: "Take my hand. I want to be your friend. I'm not going to let anything you do get in the way, so let's begin again." It really *is* that simple.

This same pattern works in human relationships. We start where we are, not where we wish we were, and we say to the person who hurt us, "I forgive you." Or: "Please forgive me. I want to be your friend (or husband, or wife, or son, or daughter or parent) again. Can we start all over?" We resist the urge to retaliate.

The miracle of forgiveness doesn't deny what happened in the past, but it does prevent bad feelings from blocking the way to a new start. Forgiveness is seldom easy, but it will take a huge weight off your back!

My Action Step

The act of forgiving is like getting rid of poison from within our souls! Since forgiving is purely a choice, if you have resentment toward someone, ask God for His help and then do your part by choosing to forgive them. You will soon find a sense of freedom in your inner being.

God's Encouraging Word

"Make allowances for each other's faults, and forgive anyone who offends you. Remember, the Lord forgave you, so you must forgive others." – Colossians 3:13, *New Living Translation*

Prayer

God, it hasn't been easy for me to forgive people who have hurt me in the past. But I want to be freed from this prison of anger and hostility and bitterness. You forgive me totally, Jesus, so I promise to do my best to forgive people who have wronged me. But I will need your help! Amen.

Day 23, "God Told Me Everything Is Going to Be OK!"

God cares for people we love even when we aren't able to do everything that we want for them.

Our oldest son is a documentary film producer living with his family on the East Coast.

Recently, I came across a note my wife had written to our son when he turned 30, telling about some family events that occurred many years earlier. I share this very personal story with you in order to demonstrate that God knows our needs, even before we verbalize them, and He is well able to take care of these needs and concerns.

Dear Steve, my mom always told me that there is something very special about your first born. It's true. In a matter of a few painful hours I was catapulted into a new category: MOTHER. It is a title filled with incredible love, spoken and unspoken dreams, and almost overwhelming responsibility for a helpless creature. Our lives had been forever changed.

And you were the most laid-back, happy-go-lucky, roll-with-the-punches kid! You have many times heard the story of how dad would come home from a night meeting and, having missed you, would wake you up from a deep sleep to play. You obligingly grinned and laughed and "talked" to your daddy until he put you back in the crib. Within minutes you were back to sleep without a complaint at the interruption.

I remember when you were nine and in fourth grade. It became evident that our time in Memphis was coming to an end. Dad had just accepted a great job in Tulsa, and we planned to leave near the end of

January. You had come to this house and this city when you were four-and-a-half, so more than half of your life had been spent here. You had your school friends, your soccer and football teams, your church buddies. You were devastated by the news that you would have to leave all this! Many nights, when I tucked you into bed, you sobbed and asked why. My "Mother heart" was in pain! The assurances I offered – "Daddy and I think this is what God wants us to do" and "You'll make new friends fast" – didn't even begin to touch your grief. After one particularly heart-rending bedtime encounter, I left your room not knowing what else to say or do.

But the next morning when you got up, you came into the kitchen with a peaceful look on your face. I could tell that something had changed. You said: "Mommy, I had a dream last night. God told me everything is going to be OK!"

I'm sure this was God's way of reminding me that He loved you more than I ever could and that He would take care of you in ways far beyond what I was capable of doing!

My Action Step

I truly believe that God's heart is broken when ours is! When we are at the end of our rope, not knowing what in the world to do, Almighty God is there for us. God will take care of those we love. We just need to "let go and let God" do His work. Are you willing to take your hands from your life and let God take over? I know that sounds easier than it really is, but the payoff – if you're willing to do it – is well worth the effort.

God's Encouraging Word

(Jesus said) "Do not let your hearts be troubled. You believe in God; believe also in me." – John 14:1

"When I am afraid, I will trust in you." – Psalm 56:3

Prayer

Oh God, give me a strong and growing faith so that I may trust those I love to your amazing care. In the name of Jesus, who loves us all. Amen.

Notes

> "As for me and my household, we will serve the Lord." – Joshua 24:15

Day 24, Do It Now!

"Don't brood. Get on with living and loving. You don't have forever." – Leo Buscaglia

In his role as professor of psychology at the University of Southern California, Dr. Leo Buscaglia began every semester with a simple, but very provocative, assignment: "Assume you only have one week to live. How would you spend that time ... and why?"

As you might expect, this exercise caused some serious soul-searching. Some students said they'd spend their remaining time with their families, using this opportunity to tell them how much they loved and appreciated them.

Others vowed they would do everything possible to reconcile with significant people in their lives ... before it was too late!

Some students said that they would track down an inspiring teacher or encouraging coach to tell them how important they had been.

Others said that they would take their little brother or sister under their wing and teach them some lessons that they had learned the hard way. "Maybe this way," one wrote, "I can spare my little sister some of the agony I went through because of my determination to experiment with everything that my parents' generation considered illegal, immoral, or unethical."

Dr. Buscaglia loved reading these assignments. Before he returned the papers to the students, he wrote at the top of each one of them in bold, red letters, **"Why don't you do it now?"**

That's a great question, don't you think?

Sometimes we go through our days like we're going to live forever! But, truth is, life can be very fleeting; we just don't know how long we (or those we love) have left. Life is just too uncertain.

Is there something you know you *should* do? Do you need to speak a word of love to someone?   Or forgiveness? Or encouragement?

The best time to do it? Right now!

I have always loved this poem, "The Time is Now" (author unknown):

If you are ever going to love me,
love me now,
while I can know the sweet and tender feelings
which from true affection flow.

Love me now, while I am living.
Do not wait until I'm gone,
and then have it chiseled in marble –
warm love words on ice-cold stone.

If you have tender thoughts of me,
why not whisper them to me?

If you wait until I am sleeping, never to awaken,
there will be death between us,
and I couldn't hear you then.

So, if you love me, even a little bit,
let me know it while I am living,
so I can treasure it.

How can we experience this kind of love? By drawing close to God. God's love is unconditional. God never holds back his love. It's always available.

A lot of people use up their precious time asking, "Why isn't the world a better place?" That's just time wasted. The question to ask is, "How can I make the world better?" And that question has an answer. If you don't like the scene you're in, if you're unhappy, if you're lonely, then change your scene! Paint a new backdrop.

Obviously, some things are beyond your ability to modify, but your job is to change what is in your power to change.

What do you need to do — not next week, but right now, to demonstrate your love and change things for the better?

My Action Step

Procrastination is an easy trap to fall into! Sometimes we con ourselves into thinking that we have all the time in the world to do things, that time doesn't really matter. But we all know that there are no guarantees. Time is of the essence. If your mind and heart tell you that you need to do something, have the courage to decide to "do it now."

God's Encouraging Word

"These are evil times, so make every minute count." – Ephesians 5:16, *Contemporary English Version*

Prayer

O Lord, please help me not to procrastinate. Motivate me to use my time well. Teach me the importance of doing things that are important "sooner," not "later." Amen.

"Serve one another in love."
– Galatians 5:13

Day 25, If This Is Not the Place

Are you a member of a caring, supportive group of people? You may think you can make it by yourself, but you really can't. God created you to be involved with other people – to encourage them and to be strengthened by them as well.

When I was in college, one of my housemates owned an ugly Ford Pinto. To me, even *new* Pintos weren't beautiful cars – but this one took the cake. It was dented in several places, had serious rust damage and sported multiple paint colors. I cracked up the first time I saw the rear bumper sticker: *God is my co-pilot!*

"Good thing!" I thought to myself. I'm glad somebody was watching over my friend. He's been through some mighty difficult times with this car!

Do you ever feel that your life is like that? Even though we may be people of faith, who acknowledge the presence of God in our lives, we know that life isn't always easy. There are times when our lives get a little ugly. Joy can be a distant memory.

It's precisely in these lowest times that we need support and strength. How do we get them?

During these times of need, sometimes the Lord will meet our needs directly, but more often than not He uses other people as His instruments. Belonging to a spiritual group gives you support. You can talk about what's bothering you when you're down, and other people can help you face your problems – it's a lot easier this way than bearing the weight of your problems all alone.

I have a sincere conviction, and it only gets stronger with the passing of the years: I think that *part of the reason we struggle so much with adversity is that we don't know how to reach out to other people!* Maybe we don't feel that anyone would want to help us. Or it could be that we don't want to appear vulnerable or weak, so we don't let other people know when we need them.

That's exactly where a community of faith comes into play. You may already be involved in a church or spiritual support group – some of you behind prison walls, others in an inpatient or outpatient support group and still others in a church congregation.

One of the most powerful illustrations of this is a song written by singer and composer, Ken Medema, who happens to be blind. It's called, "If This is Not the Place":

> *If this is not the place where tears are understood,*
> *Then where shall I go to cry?*
> *And if this is not the place where my spirit can take wings,*
> *Then where shall I go to fly?*

> *I don't need another place for trying to impress you*
> *With just how good and virtuous I am.*
> *I don't need another place for always being on top of things,*
> *Everybody knows that it's a sham.*

> *I don't need another place for always wearing a smile,*
> *Even when it's not the way I feel....*
> *So if this is not a place where my questions can be heard,*
> *Then where – tell me where – shall I go to speak?*

A lawyer friend of mine in Tulsa, Oklahoma, shared this Native American prayer with me. I think it captures the essence of Medema's song.

Journey to Freedom

O God of Love and Life,
Who created us with capacity to love –
Teach us to encourage each other,
To rejoice with each other,
To wipe the tears from each other's eyes.

My Action Step

People who are working toward recovery and are involved with other strugglers on the journey know the importance of being in a caring community. Are you part of a caring, supportive group that loves God and helps each other? This kind of community can make all the difference in the world for you! God uses other people to bless our lives. The community of faith: loving, accepting, forgiving, encouraging. If you are not part of a community of faith, why don't you seek one out, give it a try? It just may be God's method of bringing love, joy and wholeness into your life!

God's Encouraging Word

"Encourage one another and build each other up, just as in fact you are doing." – 1 Thessalonians 5:11

"Don't forget to do good things for others and to share what you have with them. These are the kinds of sacrifices that please God." – Hebrews 13:16, *GOD'S WORD Translation*

Prayer

Heavenly Father, help me to understand the importance of sharing myself with others. Help me find a group of people that I can trust. Together, we can overcome many obstacles and strive to live the kind of life you desire. Amen.

"The only sure way to take fear out of living is to keep a respectful fear of God in our lives, which means to maintain a reverent attitude toward His place and influence in the scheme of things."
– Eugene Carr, *Freedom from Fear*

Day 26, Two Kinds of Fear

Fear knocked at the door. Faith answered. No one was there! – An inscription over the mantel of Hinds Head Hotel, London

Fear is a problem we all face at one time or another. The dictionary defines fear as "a distressing emotion, caused by impending danger, evil, pain, etc."

But there's a secondary definition that's totally different when applied to God! I will explain the dramatic difference shortly, but first let me give you a few examples of the first kind of fear:

First kind of fear

- I feared the past until I realized that it could no longer hurt me.
- I feared being alone until I learned to like myself.
- I feared failure until I realized that I fail only when I don't try.
- I feared rejection until I learned to have faith in myself.
- I feared pain until I learned that pain is necessary for growth.
- I feared the truth until I saw the ugliness in lies.
- I feared hate until I saw that hate was nothing more than ignorance.
- I feared death until I realized that death is not an end, but a new beginning.

Another meaning of fear – when used in connection with God

This use of the word fear doesn't refer to distressed emotions caused by the possibility of evil, pain or danger. It actually means something altogether different. The formal dictionary definition is "reverential awe toward God," but let me put it in more familiar terms. The fear of God means a sense of reverence and awe, a healthy respect that leads us to worship and obey His commands as seen in Scripture. Here are some examples:

Anyone who fears God need fear nothing else.
The fear of God kills all other fears!

Now let's compare these two definitions of fear. The reality is that only as we respect God can we find His help to overcome our fears of other people and circumstances.

Since fear is unreasonable, never try to reason with it. So-called "positive thinking" is no weapon against fear.

Only positive faith can rout the dark menace of fear and give life radiance.

My Action Step

Is there something or someone you fear? Focus on Almighty God. Think of His power. Put your faith in Him, and your fears will not be so overwhelming. In fact, they may even disappear.

God's Encouraging Word

"Perfect love drives out fear." – 1 John 4:18

"As a father has compassion on his children, so the Lord has compassion on those who fear him." – Psalm 103:13

Prayer

Lord, help me to grasp the reality of your unfailing love in my life. Once I accept that perfect love, I have nothing to fear and I can keep moving toward being free. Thank you, Lord! Amen.

Day 27, Forgive Yourself!

Why is it so hard to forgive ourselves?

I can't begin to tell you how many people I've known over the years who have had a hard time forgiving themselves for things they've said or done or failed to do. Their attitude seems to be, "Forgive everyone except yourself!"

Why would anyone choose to imprison himself or herself with guilt?

I don't want to be naive. I understand that self-forgiveness is often difficult. I sometimes struggle with this too. We've all made stupid decisions which have hurt other people as well as ourselves. And I think that forgiving ourselves is especially hard when we've hurt someone that we love. Since they're close to us, their very presence often reminds us of the hurt that we caused them.

But let's be honest: sometimes we hurt people, and we aren't even aware of it. This often happens because we just got too busy or preoccupied or we forgot to do something we said we'd do. Good people sometimes hurt others unintentionally. That doesn't mean we are evil!

Take an honest look at your past. It may be painful, but you've got to do it. You need to confront the skeletons rattling around in your closet. (We all have them!) Next, take all your failures and regrets and say out loud: "God, now I realize that you want me to learn from my sins and shortcomings, and grow spiritually, so I can become the person you want me to be."

Then, most importantly, invite God into your memory of the past. Let Him in. As you remember the wrongs that you've done and the hurts you've caused, embrace the unconditional acceptance and total forgiveness of the God who loves you.

God doesn't focus on your past failures. Instead, He wants to liberate you so that your future will be filled with right decisions and fewer failures. God says, "I love you. I don't condemn you. I forgive you."

The Apostle Paul wasn't unaware of his past imperfections; their memory was very real to him. Here was a man who stood by and more or less supervised people as they stoned Stephen to death simply for preaching about Jesus Christ (Acts 7). But in time, by God's grace, Paul learned how to live by this motto: "I forget what lies behind and I strain forward to what lies ahead" (Philippians 3:13).

My Action Step

Paul gives great advice. Pray and work toward confessing your past so that you can be freed from it. Most importantly, if you haven't already done so, reach out and begin a personal relationship with Jesus Christ. Humbly ask Him to forgive your past sins, actions, and errors of omission (the sin of failing to do what you ought to have done). Invite Him into your life. Be encouraged by the Bible verse that follows, and then pray to incorporate these liberating truths into your soul.

God's Encouraging Word

"So now there is no condemnation for those who belong to Christ Jesus." – Romans 8:1, *New Living Translation*

Prayer

Dear Lord, knowing that you have forgiven my past helps to understand your unconditional love for me. Now, as I hang onto that wonderful reality, help me to forgive myself, too. I know this isn't easy, so thank you for this gift and for walking forward with me on my journey. Amen.

Day 28, Keep Your Fork!

"The dwelling of God is with men, and he will live with them. They will be his people, and God himself will be with them and be their God. He will wipe every tear from their eyes. There will be no death or mourning or crying or pain, for the old order of things has passed away." – Revelation 21:3b-4

Roger W. Thomas wrote the following story in 1994. Since then, it has made its way around the world via the Internet. It's about a young woman who had been diagnosed with a terminal illness and given just three months to live.

As she was getting her things in order, she contacted her pastor and asked that he come to her house to discuss her final wishes. She told him which songs she wanted sung at the memorial service, which Scriptures she would like read and even which outfit she wanted to be buried in.

Just as the pastor was preparing to leave, the young woman suddenly remembered something very important to her. "There's one more thing," she said enthusiastically.

"What's that, Joanie?" the pastor replied.

"This is very important," she insisted. "I want to be buried with a fork in my right hand!" she continued.

He stood there confused, not knowing quite what to say.

So she explained: "My grandmother once told me this story, and I've tried to pass along its message to people I love and those who are in need of encouragement. I've attended many church socials and potluck dinners in my time and thinking back on them now, I recall that moment when the dishes of the main course were being cleared away; and inevitably, someone would lean forward and say, 'Remember to keep your fork.' It was my favorite part because I knew that something better was coming – like velvety chocolate cake or deep-dish apple pie. So I just want people to see me there in that casket with a fork in my hand, and I want them to wonder, 'What's with the fork?'

"Then I want you to tell them: 'Keep your fork ... the best is yet to come!'"

The minister's eyes welled up with tears as he hugged Joanie goodbye. He knew this might be one of the last times he would see her alive. He also knew that she had a better grasp of heaven than he did!

She knew that something better was coming!

At the funeral people walked by the casket and, of course, they all saw the fork in her right hand. Again and again the pastor heard the question, "What's the meaning of the fork?" He just smiled, and didn't say anything.

Later, during his brief message he told the people about the conversation he had had with Joanie. He told them about the fork and what it symbolized for her.

So the next time you reach down for your fork, let it remind you that the best is yet to come!

My Action Step

Stay focused on life's end reward, which is eternal life with Jesus Christ. Having this confidence brings complete peace to our hearts, even when we are facing hard times.

God's Encouraging Word

"Eye has not seen, ear has not heard, nor has it entered into the human heart what God has prepared for those who love him." – 1 Corinthians 2:9

Prayer

Father, you have prepared a place for me in heaven! Help me to stay focused through adversity, knowing that, through faith in Christ, I have eternal life with you. Amen.

Notes

"Forgiveness is a miracle. Through forgiveness, what is broken is made whole again; what is soiled is made clean again." – Anon

Day 29, Not Defeat, Victory!

Do you feel like you live in a dungeon of hopelessness? You do NOT have to stay there! Jesus Christ can unlock the door and lead you into a new day of hope!

One of the great military battles of all time was the Battle of Waterloo in Belgium, in 1815. The British forces were led by the Duke of Wellington and the French forces by Napoleon. The English, who had lived for twenty years with the dread that Napoleon might invade them, anxiously awaited news of the outcome of this battle.

There were no electronic communication devices then – not even a telegraph. Word was sent from the seaport on the English Channel to London by flag men stationed in towers located at regular intervals along the English coast.

The boat from Belgium arrived in the English port with news of the outcome. The first signalman spelled out: "W-E-L-L-I-N-G-T-O-N-D-E-F-E-A-T-E-D." This message was sent along the line. However, in London, a thick, dense fog had rolled in, making it impossible to see any additional signals that might have been sent.

London society was shocked by the news: The British had lost the battle! They had been defeated by the great Napoleon. They were filled with despair, hopelessness. It was only a matter of time before they were occupied and maybe enslaved.

I recalled this story as I thought about people I know who have been defeated in life. Change the name "Wellington" to your own and say, "_____ defeated." Do you ever feel that way? Do you feel a heavy weight of loss or failure or guilt for what you have done? Are you depressed thinking you'll never get ahead?

If you feel defeated by life, then hear the rest of the story.

The next day the fog in London lifted, and the last part of the message came through. The message now read, "W-E-L-L-I-N-G-T-O-N-D-E-F-E-A-T-E-D-T-H-E-E-N-E-M-Y." Not defeat but victory! Despair, depression, and hopelessness immediately gave way to celebration, laughter, and hope!

Now insert the name Jesus Christ into the sentence: "Jesus Christ defeated the enemy!" Think about it: Every conceivable bad thing you've ever done or even imagined has been defeated by God's love, through Christ, when He died on the cross. As a result, every sadness you've ever experienced can be turned 180 degrees into a time of joy. Jesus has come to wipe away the tears from your eyes. Every vicious action you've committed has been forgiven by the One who came to give life in full measure.

All of us have experienced what is called an "Ohnosecond." An ohnosecond is that smallest fraction of time in which you realize that you've just made a BIG mistake. But our faith proclaims that Christ has come to heal your mistakes and give you a second chance!

Hope for the future is real for those who put their faith in God's gift of love, Jesus Christ.

My Action Step

Take an ordinary key that fits into a lock. [If that's not possible, you will need to use your imagination.] Hold the key in your hand. Now put it into the lock and turn it. As you do so, think about the fact that Jesus is the key for you to be released from the bondage of depression, sadness, loneliness, and hopelessness. As the key turns in the lock, take a courageous step of faith and give yourself to Christ. Ask God to free you from the mistakes of the past. Invite Him to fill your mind and heart with new life, new energy, and new hope. As you do, He will bless you richly!

God's Encouraging Word

"Every child of God can defeat the world, and our faith is what gives us this victory." – 1 John 5:4, *Contemporary English Version*

"But thank God! He gives us the victory over sin and death through our Lord Jesus Christ." – 1 Corinthians 15:57

Prayer

God of hope, help me to find the key that releases your love into my heart and soul today. Give me courage so that I may make the leap across the chasm of doubt, despair, guilt, shame and sorrow and put my faith in your Son, Jesus Christ. Amen.

Notes

"No eye has seen, no ear has heard, and no mind has imagined what God has prepared for those who love him." – 1 Corinthians 2:9, *New Living Translation*

Day 30, God Loves You

There is nothing you could ever do to make God love you more! And there is nothing you could ever do to make God love you less!

God's love is unconditional. There's absolutely nothing you can do to change that fact. God loves you. Period. End of story.

The Bible says, "God loved the people of the world so much that he gave his only Son, so that everyone who has faith in him will have eternal life and never die" (John 3:16, *Contemporary English Version*). God loves you so much that He sent His only Son to die a most horrific death, so that your sins could be forgiven. Jesus, knowing the pain and anguish that awaited Him, willingly died on the cross so that you might have everlasting life. This is love with a capital "L." God loves you in ways that you might never fully understand. But it's not necessary to understand. Just accept it. Wouldn't it be best to get rid of doubt and start believing?

We've all done things that we're not proud of. Maybe you broke some law of society, and now you're paying the price for it. Perhaps you continue to struggle with the bonds of addiction, and you're in pain because you know that you're hurting not only yourself, but also people who love you. Or maybe you've fallen into the trap of vengeance, wishing terrible things upon someone who has hurt you.

When we place our faith in what Christ has done for us on the cross, God takes our sins and buries them in the deepest ocean. Then *He forgets all about them.* That's how much He loves you. No matter what you've done, God doesn't even remember. Maybe you need to learn to forgive yourself, too!

The Bible says it best: "How great is God's love for all who fear him? Greater than the distance between heaven and earth" (Psalm 103:11, *Contemporary English Version*).

God's love will always be unconditional – you can't add to it or subtract from it – but you have to take certain steps to enable that love to work its wonders in your life. First, you have to believe that God exists. Then you have to go one step further: reach out with faith and accept His love. If you don't, the net result is that you will wall Him out of your life. To experience the fullness of God's love, all you need to do is accept the fact that Jesus came to earth to die for your sins and believe in Him in order to experience eternal life. Then, once you've entered the Christian life, you need to lean to grow in obedience to Him. Accepting Christ as your personal Savior, and turning your back on your old ways, will literally open the flood gates of God's love!

If you can fully comprehend how deeply you are loved by God, you will never feel alone again.

My Action Step

Give yourself in faith to the God who says that there's nothing you can do that could ever make God love you more or less than He already does. Accept that unconditional love and, in gratitude, offer your life to the Lord. Maybe you don't see yourself as a particularly religious person. That's OK – just give as much of yourself as you can, right now, to the Lord.

God's Encouraging Word

[Jesus said:] "If you hold to my teaching, you are really my disciples. Then you will know the truth, and the truth will set you free." – John 8:31-32

"Anyone who belongs to Christ is a new person. The past is forgotten, and everything is new." – 2 Corinthians 5:17, *Contemporary English Version*

A Suggested Prayer

If you are truly sorry for your sins, God will forgive you. He will cleanse you from all your guilt and give you a new life. You will never be the same again! I encourage you to pray this simple prayer of invitation:

Father, when I picked up this book, I desperately wanted to be free. I had my own ideas of how to get there, but they weren't working. I've done things that have haunted me and hurt others. I've had things going on in my life that I regret, and I've done things that I regret. I've come to realize that I have been in bondage to my own attitudes and actions, which fall far short of your standard.

*But in reading "Journey to Freedom," I have come to believe that my human efforts have been powerless to deal with the problem of my sin, that **freedom from the penalty of sin** only comes through faith in Jesus Christ.*

*I've also seen that **freedom from the power of sin** only happens through a growing faith in Christ.*

Lord God, just as I've learned that I must depend upon Christ alone to deliver me from the penalty of sin, I know that I need to learn to depend upon Christ to deliver me from the power of sin in my everyday life.

Lord, take out of my life what shouldn't be there. Replace my self-absorbed thoughts and selfish desires with your thoughts and desires for me.

Father, thank you that you loved me enough that you sent Jesus to die for me! And I also thank you that you love me enough right now to keep me from staying the way I am! Please develop in my heart a burning desire to become the person you want me to be.

Help me to live as a new person. I know that I will never be perfect, but now I understand that I am perfectly loved and totally forgiven. I have finally found freedom and hope because of your perfect love. I pray in the name of your Son, my Lord Jesus Christ, who died for me and now lives in me! Amen

"So if the Son sets you free, you are truly free."
– John 8:36, *New Living Translation*

We would appreciate it so much if you would turn to the last page and read A Final Word. Then go to the Response Page and let us know your impressions of *Journey to Freedom*.

Acknowledgements

With heart-felt thanks to:

Rev. Cam Abell, who has served for 16-years with Good News Jail & Prison Ministry as a chaplain, as a Regional Director supervising chaplains, and as the Director of Training. Cam continues to train chaplains and volunteers nationally and internationally. He has made a number of valuable suggestions for this printing. How grateful I am to have had another set of eyes to provide clarity and freshness.

Dr. Robert S. Thomson, gifted editor, erudite scholar, prolific author and my brother in the Faith. This is the third book that we have collaborated on. Robert began as a doubter and has taken the journey of faith that I am describing in this book.

My son, Steve, who is also a gifted editor. His words continue to echo in my ears, "Dig deeper, Dad; dig deeper."

My son, Brian, for his creative work on the cover design. Brian is a graphic designer with remarkable skills.

Rev. Chuck Walker, retired correctional chaplain with more than 20 years experience. Chuck knows our audience, and his wisdom has been profoundly helpful.

Church members and friends who took the time to read through the manuscript and make constructive suggestions: Carol and Gordon B., Chris Bryant, Linda Munro, Joan O., Jim Parrish, Rev. Ralph Spencer, Dorree Sullivan, and Corrine Yates. And to Penny Eighmy, who contributed several of the prayers.

My dear friends, the Council at Community Church of Joy, who gave me time off to write this book and encouraged me along the way: John Albin, Bill B., Cathy Chappell, Joel Crouch, Dick G., Gail Lawson, Jim Parrish, Fred Russell, and Bob Rain. And my friends, Council members at my other church, Shenandoah Bible Fellowship: Marlene and Bill Swedeen and Marilyn and Harland Wold.

Chapter 12 was written in collaboration with my brother, Dave, a retired minister who lives with his wife in a retirement community in Central Florida. Chapter 29 was written along with my friend, Dr. Ralph Spencer, a retired pastor of the United Church of Canada, and now a member of our congregation in California. Ralph also suggested several outstanding illustrations for which I am most grateful. Chapter 30 was written in collaboration with my friend, Chris Bryant, a member of our congregation and an executive search consultant.

To all those who have contributed financially to *Journey to Freedom*: your generosity, along with your friendship and prayers, are deeply appreciated. You have shared your financial gifts so that others may take this most important journey, a journey with our Lord!

Finally, I can't express fondly enough my appreciation for the board of "Journey to Freedom Foundation"! You, dear friends, have worked countless hours, giving of yourselves, so that God's love could be shared with people you don't even know! I am grateful to Cathy and Skip Chappell, Connie Dorst, Penny Eighmy, Linda Munro, Deanie Parrish, Mary Swink and Chaplain Chuck Walker.

Testimonials

"When I got locked up I was literally hopeless. I fantasized about suicide. I was taking medication for anxiety and depression. Today, I want God to be the reason I am well. He has been good and faithful to help me get to a point where hope has been restored. I've still got a way to go – and I strongly believe your book has been given me through intervention of God."

S.M., S. Texas Intermediate Sanctions Unit, TX

"When I tried to hang myself in county jail, and I told God to let me die, He did. I really died that day, and I never realized it. The old is gone and the new is working every day. When I got your book I just couldn't put it down. I still have a lot of bitterness, loneliness and heartache. But I'm dealing with it through the Lord."

W.A., Ellis Unit, TX

"I am seldom very impressed by what I read, but *Journey to Freedom* is first-class and God-inspired! I opened the pages and it 'glowed.' I am using Dr. Dorst's book with my ministry to my staff as well as with our inmates. Only God knows what good will come from this book!"

Chaplain Wayne Horton, Jim Rudd Unit, Brownfield, TX

"My reason for this letter is because I fell in love with this book called *Journey to Freedom*. Well, because of me reading that book I have rededicated my life to our Lord Jesus Christ and it has helped me move forward in life and learn to forgive myself and others."

A.M., Indio, CA

"*Journey to Freedom* is a well-lit path of hope for anyone who is struggling with feeling abandoned by God. Dr. Dorst's words provide important keys to unlocking the inner chains of shame and guilt. This book is clear, concrete, non-judgmental and firmly rooted in the wisdom of Scripture. I love this book! We have ordered 1,000 copies for use within our jails."

Chaplain Dave Robinson, Elmwood Prison, Milpitas, CA

"I am a 35 year old man who is addicted to meth. This drug and many poor decisions have caused much pain and shame. When I was arrested this time I was ready to throw in the towel. [This man's chaplain explained that he was referring to hanging himself in his cell, an epidemic among inmates.] Then one day someone slid your book under my cell door. I don't even know who it was. As I've read each story, action step, God's encouraging word and prayer, I've continued to gain faith and hope again. Although I still consider myself a mess, I know that I'm just a blessed mess who needs God in my life."

C.S., Milpitas, CA

"For the longest time I had begged loved ones, friends, and family for their forgiveness for the things I've done wrong, and although they would always say 'It's OK,' I would never feel better. I was asking the wrong Person! Then, when I started to read JTF I instantly felt not just better about myself but better about my life and the new direction I had just taken. I thought forgiveness was something of mere words. I now know TRUE forgiveness, God's forgiveness, and what a blessing it is."

J.J., recovering alcoholic and drug addict

"Thank you for your encouragement and support in reaching out to the lost, hurting, and the dying in the name of our Lord Jesus."

Captain Jerry Esqueda, Salvation Army, El Centro, CA

"I know God has forgiven me; I get that. But your book hit right on my issue: forgiving myself. One bad choice outweighs 20 years of good – the good thing is I am back with God. The book was a great reminder that I am not alone."

Former correctional officer, now serving time

"I would like to take my experience with this book and share it with the world. There is a God and he truly loves me. I am going to introduce my children and family to my new life."

W.L., Dublin, CA

"In *Journey to Freedom*, Dr. Rich Dorst presents in short daily reading format, excellent recommendations for application to everyday living for people who are incarcerated or in recovery programs and who seek rehabilitation. He speaks to the real and felt needs of those who are often forgotten but in the eyes of God are equal to the rest of us.

This book is easy to read, clear, and compelling, and focuses primarily on reconciling the spiritual component of a person which is necessary for a successful and lasting re-integration into society.

This is a must read, not only for the incarcerated, but also for all those who have employment related responsibilities to watch over them and anyone else who wishes to help them."

Peter J Falk. B.A, LL.B. Q.C.
Chair, Prison Fellowship Canada

"I wish *Journey to Freedom* had been written when I was serving as a correctional chaplain. It would have been a big help in my ministry, giving practical help for prisoners who want to make real changes in their lives. Over the years I would have given out thousands of copies as a guide and encouragement for those seeking forgiveness and a new beginning. I believe that most inmates really want to change but often can't admit it even to themselves. They need to know that God cares and that we care. This book is not only for inmates but for anyone who wants to make real changes in their lives."

Rev. Chuck Walker, correctional chaplain, Santa Clara, CA

Dr. Dorst has discovered a format that will resonate with readers: real-life stories and reflection (taking time to absorb and think about what was just read); My Action Step (personalizing the message); God's Encouraging Word (I'm a big fan of encouragement!); and Prayer (connecting with God). *Journey to Freedom* is very readable. The stories easily hold one's attention. It is written for everyone! For staff and volunteers to use this in a prison setting, each one (including myself) can relate to the life-changing and important values that are being instilled. It levels the playing field! I realize it was written especially for those in prison and those suffering from addictions, but it is really for us all."

Rev. Sadie Pounder, associate pastor, Holy Trinity Lutheran Church, Lancaster, PA; chaplain and author of *Prison Theology: A Theology of Liberation, Hope and Justice (Dialog, Fall, 2008)*

"*Journey to Freedom* will be a very useful ministry into men's lives in prison. You should know that at least 5 men read the same book sent behind bars."

C.W., Ione, CA

"I find *Journey to Freedom* simple to read, and it easily brings you to its purpose in each chapter. I especially appreciate My Action Step at the conclusion of each daily reading."

Bill Luttrell, Divisional Commander,
Salvation Army, San Diego, CA

"I was given a book by my chaplain. At the end of day one reading I was sitting in my cell alone in tears. But wait, I was not alone. Me and my Lord were crying together. My journey since then has been easier to say the least. I would give the book to anyone, not just folks in jail."

M.S., Elmwood Correctional Center, Milpitas, CA

"I must say that before someone handed me your book I was still lost. But once I picked it up and read it I found a new love in my life to wanna live. I have a lot of demons in my closet and am filled with these demons everyday, yet I've now learned that I must be strong and let God take away my pain."

G.K., Camp Hill, PA

"I have a friend who came across the book, *Journey to Freedom* here in Indio County Jail. Well, my friend reads to 11 of us every night, and we'd love to have a copy of our own."

A.D., Indio, CA

"It's kinda hard for me to express my gratitude for this powerful book. It arrived at just the right time. While I was in the darkest moments of my life. It blessed me with new hope and a reason to keep going. Your ability to mix sincerity, love, hope, and compassion with humor is what I appreciate most. The stories are quick and to the point. The action steps are motivating, the God's encouraging word is…well, encouraging! And the prayers are so powerful."   E, Santa Clara, CA

Response

We would be honored if you would take a minute and let us know what *Journey to Freedom* has meant to you.

1. What did you like most about this book?

2. How has your life been affected by your reading *Journey to Freedom?* How is it helping you to deal with problems or struggles in your life or in your personal faith journey?

3. What suggestions do you have to improve the quality of this book?

4. Would you like to add any other comments?

Thank you so much for taking the time and effort
to complete this form.
Please place in an envelope and mail to:
Dr. Rich Dorst
Journey to Freedom Foundation,
P.O. Box 3344
Palm Desert, CA 92261

A Final Word

Those of us associated with Journey to Freedom Foundation are delighted that you have read this book! We sincerely hope that it has been helpful to you in your journey with God and others and that it has given you a sense of hope, meaning and purpose.

Contact us at: journeytofreedom@earthlink.net.

If you feel moved to contribute to our ministry to help us print and distribute additional copies, your generosity would be greatly appreciated. You may send a check to Journey to Freedom Foundation, PO Box 3344, Palm Desert, CA 92261. All gifts are fully tax-deductible.

Blessings,

Cathy Chappell,
Foundation President

JTF

FOUNDATION
journeytofreedomfoundation.org

Journey to Freedom